WHEAT-FREE COOKING

WHEAT-FREE COOKING

Practical Help for the Home Cook

Rita Greer

SOUVENIR PRESS

First published 1995 by Souvenir Press Ltd.,
43 Great Russell Street, London WC1B 3PA
and simultaneously in Canada

Reprinted 1996, 1998, 2000

ISBN 0 285 63238 8

Photoset by Rowland Phototypesetting Ltd.,
Bury St Edmunds, Suffolk
Printed in Great Britain by
The Guernsey Press Co. Ltd., Guernsey, Channel Islands.

Contents

CHAPTER 1

Wheat and the Western Diet

Wheat is man's premier grain. It features in the daily diet of most people in the Western world—in bread, breakfast cereals, pasta, biscuits, cakes, crispbreads and many other foods. What makes it so important, and why do some people need to live without it?

Combine wheat grains with soil, water and sunlight, and the result is a harvest of many more grains that are easy to store, will keep for a long time and can be made into all kinds of nourishing foods. The whole grain or parts of it can be processed to create a variety of flours, bran and wheat germ, because each grain (wheat berry) comprises an outer layer of fibre, a store of starch and, in the centre, the miraculous little germ designed to reproduce—wheat germ.

From a nutritional point of view wheat is a valued food,

containing carbohydrate, protein, a little fat, vitamins, minerals and fibre, but its true worth lies in the *gluten* it contains. No other grain will make a delicate sponge, a crisp biscuit or crispbread, pastry that melts in the mouth, a large loaf of bread, crusty rolls, light scones, soft crumble or rich fruit cake. All these are possible because of gluten—a special rubbery kind of protein which enables an elastic kind of dough to be made that will rise and double in size, keep its shape and hold up fruit, and enclose liquids or moist food. All this, combined with an excellent flavour, endless supply and low price—little wonder that wheat is known as the 'king of crops'.

WHEAT ALLERGY AND INTOLERANCE

Although, because it is so widely used, and in so many forms, it is tempting to think of wheat as wholly beneficial, for a small percentage of the population it represents a harmful element in their daily food. Wheat is now thought to be the major allergen (allergy-provoking substance) in the Western diet. Symptoms vary and may involve one or several of the following:

1 *Eyes*: watery, itching, swollen, red, blurred vision, tired, sore, heavy feeling in eyelids.
2 *Nose*: runny nose, sinusitis, sneezing, itching, excessive mucus, burning, blocked nose.
3 *Ears*: ringing in the ears, soreness, earache, loss of hearing, burning sensations, itching.
4 *Head*: feeling faint and dizzy, heavy feeling, headaches, migraine.
5 *Throat and mouth*: soreness, swollen tongue, mouth ulcers, sore gums, loss of taste, hoarseness, cough, choking fits, itching of the roof of the mouth, bad breath.

6 *Heart and lungs*: pains in the chest, rapid heart beat, palpitations, asthma, congestion in the chest, tight feeling across chest, shallow breathing, excessive sighing, breathlessness, catarrh.

7 *Gastro-intestinal*: feeling of nausea, vomiting, diarrhoea, constipation, stomach cramps, swollen stomach, bloated feeling after eating, feeling 'full-up' long after meals, pains in the stomach, flatulence, poor appetite, cravings for foods, dyspepsia.

8 *Skin*: rashes, hives, easily marked skin, eczema, excessively pale colour, inexplicable bruises, dermatitis, itching, soreness, excessive sweating, redness, sores, acne.

9 *Other physical symptoms*: weakness, fatigue, cramp, convulsions (extremely rare), cold hands and feet, shivering fits, nervousness, flushing, trembling, aches and pains in the joints, swelling of limbs, face, hands, feet and ankles, swollen joints, aches and pains in the muscles, constant feeling of hunger, gorging with food, oedema, hayfever, obesity.

10 *Pyschological and behaviour symptoms*: anxiety, attacks of panic, depression, hyperactivity, apathy, restlessness, irritability, daydreaming, speech difficulties, confusion, poor concentration, general feeling of misery, mood swings, aggressive behaviour, unreasonable giggling or weeping, couldn't-care-less attitude, excessive sleeping, insomnia.

From this long list you can see that confusion might easily arise regarding diagnosis, and this is probably why the medical profession is so shy of diagnosing food allergy— there are several possible explanations for each symptom. Take, for instance, headaches. These could be caused by eye-strain, tension, not enough sleep, migraine, a head injury, constipation or a much more serious complaint.

With such a battery of symptoms it is not surprising to find a wheat-free diet being used to try and control several illnesses or symptoms—M.E. (myalgic encephalomyelitis or post viral syndrome), IBS (irritable bowel syndrome), Crohn's disease, MS (multiple sclerosis), Gulf War syndrome, autism, dyslexia, migraine, arthritis, inexplicable skin rashes, aches and pains; headaches, fatigue, depression, or any or several of the symptoms listed above. Some seem to be complaints for which there is no known cure. However, this does not mean that wheat should be blamed for all illnesses. **Any persistent symptoms are best investigated by a qualified medical practitioner.** If a cure is not possible, then any alleviation of symptoms is worth having to lessen the misery and discomfort of persistent ill health, and this is why people try a wheat-free diet. It is often the first to be suggested by practitioners of alternative and complementary medicine, who are more inclined to treat the patient as a whole rather than just addressing the allergy symptoms. Wheat plays such a major role in our daily diet that where allergies are suspected the culprit is more likely to be wheat than any other grain or food.

As wheat can turn up in the most unlikely foods, excluding it means removing not only the foods that obviously contain it—bread, cakes, pasta and biscuits—but also many others that contain small amounts, such as gravies, sauces and soups. This has the effect of nutritionally unbalancing the normal diet to the extent that it becomes unworkable. To give you some idea of how much wheat is in our diet, look at the second and third columns of Table 2, pages 32–9.

USES OF WHEAT FLOUR

Flour made from wheat has many uses—for thickening, binding, dusting and making liquids creamy. You will find it used for thickening gravies, soups, sauces, casseroles and stews; for dusting biscuits, crispbreads, breads and baking tins; for rolling out pastry and coating food before frying; as a base for baking powder; added to blancmange, custard and desserts; to 'stretch' pepper, curry powder, spices and so on.

Wheat flour bread is used for stuffings, breadcrumb coatings, bulking out burgers, pastes, pâtés, sausages and pie or pasty fillings, summer pudding, bread and butter pudding, toast, fried bread, croûtons, toppings; for thickening soups; to make 'rusk', itself a thickener and dry powder base when ground.

Wheat flour biscuits are used for cake and pie bases, flans, toppings and confectionery.

Wheat starch may be used to make MSG (Monosodium Glutamate, a flavour enhancer), and communion wafers.

Brands
Some brands of food may contain wheat while a similar product of another brand does not—for example, tomato sauce. For this reason it is easier to prepare food at home rather than trudge around the shops looking for a wheat-free commercial version. See Table 2 (pp. 32–9) for more details.

THE BATTLE AGAINST WHEAT

Wheat in Processed Foods
During the processing of wheat-free foods, wheat may be added. Although they start life on the wheat-free list, it does not take much for them to be transferred to the unsafe list, to be avoided.

Any food which has been processed—canned, frozen, cooked, baked, fried, mixed, liquidised, dusted, coated, minced, bottled, ground or shredded—has had the opportunity to have wheat added. *Plain, simple foods are always the safest.*

Reading the Label

Put yourself in the position of a manufacturer. You have a product which needs to be thickened: business sense will tell you to use the cheapest starch available. Usually it will be wheat, but there may be times when you cannot obtain this or when another starch is cheaper. Also, you may not wish your competitors to know what you have used. Your printed list of ingredients on the label may therefore show any of the following: *wholegrain, flour, starch, modified starch, rusk, cereal protein, cereal, edible starch, food starch, binder, vegetable protein, thickening or thickener.*

All these could indicate wheat or a wheat byproduct. On the other hand they might not mean wheat at all. (Only if *wheat meal* or *wheat protein* appear on the list can you assume they definitely contain wheat.)

There are other thickeners—cornstarch, cornflour, rye flour and barley flour, although the last two are rarely used as they are expensive compared to wheat and corn/maize products.

Contamination

Sometimes wheat is used not actually in the food product itself but in its manufacture, for example, to dust tins or baking sheets, rather than the more costly rye, barley and oatmeal. However, wheat is still unlikely to appear on the ingredients list. A crispbread packet label might list 'rye flour, water, salt' but the food could be contaminated by the dusting wheat used to prevent the crispbreads sticking together. Was the rye flour milled in the same grain mill as wheat flour? The only clue is an allergic reaction to the supposed wheat-free product. Although this is not a problem for the average allergy sufferer it could be serious for someone acutely allergic to wheat.

Contamination may also occur in the home when wheat flour or wheat products are handled in the same area as others. Take a look in your toaster. Unless you have dismantled it and cleaned it thoroughly after the last piece of toast was made in it, it will be contaminated by wheat breadcrumbs.

Have you ever seen inside a bakery? A cloud of wheat dust hangs over the whole area. It is also on the baker's overalls, under his fingernails, in his hair, on his face, all over the equipment, the walls, the floor and so on. There will be sacks of wheat flour and much-used and seldom changed baking tins. Common sense will tell you that there is no hope of buying any food from a wheat bakery which is completely wheat-free and any person with a wheat allergy should avoid bakeries and mills. For some people, just breathing in the dust is enough to set off an allergic reaction.

Control
Please don't be daunted by all this information. Help is at hand in the rest of this book. If you are prepared to cook at home, 95 per cent of the problems will disappear and your main source of trouble will probably be supermarkets and restaurants.

If you are cooking for someone else or the rest of the family it is easy to make a mistake and then feel guilty because you have failed. If you yourself are the wheat allergic and you make a mistake, retribution comes with the return of symptoms—sometimes learning has to be done the hard way.

No one should expect to be in control of the situation immediately: a wheat-free diet is not like a slimming diet that can be broken and then resumed without harm. However, we are all human—even a genius can make mistakes. Know-how is all-important and a practical approach from home really is by far the easiest solution.

Dietary Mistakes

In the recipe chapters the ingredients likely to be suspect are emphasised to draw your attention to them. You will also find information there explaining why particular ingredients need special care. By working through the recipes you will gradually build up the knowledge you need to cope with a wheat-free diet.

If you are keeping both wheat-containing and wheat-free foods in the same kitchen, mark the special ones in some way to avoid mistakes. Cut up address labels, or you can buy small, coloured stick-on labels from stationers and some supermarkets. You should find that good kitchen shops stock labels with special glue to stick on food for the freezer (ordinary stick-on labels will fall off in the frosty atmosphere).

Approaches

There are two approaches to going on a special diet. One is to find out all you can about it, calmly make adjustments and rely largely on home cooking and food preparation. The other, calculated to make your family, friends and colleagues run out of patience, is to spend hours shopping and parting with a lot of money for strange foods, just because they are wheat-free, which you probably won't enjoy. Combine this with doing the rounds of local eating places which have never heard of, and certainly don't intend to cope with, a wheat-free diet, and is it any wonder that life becomes difficult?

Budget and Shopping

Assuming your budget is the same for the new diet as it was for your previous one, then the more basic, unprocessed foods that you can use the better. There is no need to spend a small fortune on exotic ingredients or to patronise specialist shops.

You will probably find shopping in supermarkets a nuisance if you are used to buying processed and ready-made foods. It takes a little longer to shop if you have to keep reading ingredients labels. A little notebook, preferably indexed, will be invaluable here. Once you have found a suitable brand or brands of foods that you need on a regular basis, write the name in the notebook and always take it with you when you go shopping for food, or give it to someone who is shopping for you. Keep it up to date and life will be easier, but still check the labels in case the ingredients have changed. Also include your own ingredients list of thickeners (see *Reading the Label*, p. 12) for reference. The more fresh fruit, vegetables, plain meat and fish you buy, the fewer problems you will experience. Junk food is your real danger!

Starting

Use this book to get started sensibly. If a wheat-free diet is the answer to your health problem, then the rewards for persevering will be positive and worthwhile. Balance your diet using the information in the next chapter to make it as nutritious as possible and try not to be too ambitious to start with.

In the recipe chapters you will find many ordinary, well-known foods changed just slightly to make them wheat-free; you are unlikely to notice the difference and their very familiarity will feel reassuring and help build confidence in the new regime.

There is one short list of basic foods it would be useful to know by heart. They form the basis of a wheat-free diet:

fruit/vegetables
meat/fish
cheese/eggs
rice/oats/rye/barley
sugar/milk/nuts—all PLAIN

Gluten-free

A note here about the term 'gluten-free'. Sometimes, but not always, this can indicate that a product is also wheat-free. However, many products labelled 'gluten-free' can be wheat starch itself. So don't fall into the trap of assuming gluten-free automatically means wheat-free—it doesn't. See Useful Information, p. 122.

CHAPTER 2

Nutrition for a Wheat-Free Diet

Removing all forms of wheat from your diet can be a traumatic affair if care is not taken to re-balance your food intake. It is quite common to experience a drastic loss of weight at first, simply because it means cutting out so many of the popular and convenience foods we enjoy. To remove all these at a stroke is nothing short of a disaster to a person dependent on them. So, having established that the situation is not to be taken lightly, your first step must be to reorganise your shopping, cooking and kitchen skills.

Your greatest difficulty may be the gap left by wheat bread. Unfortunately, you may find yourself craving for the very food that has been causing problems. With some people, eating bread and wheat-based foods becomes a kind of addiction and avoiding them can lead to withdrawal symptoms.

17

As it will be difficult, expensive or even impossible to buy 100 per cent wheat-free bread, one of your priorities is to find a good substitute. Rye and barley flour are both nutritious but do not contain the same quality or amount of gluten to bind them that we find in wheat. Both are best blended with other flours to improve taste and baking performance. Egg white can be added to give extra elasticity to the dough, but a mixture of rye, barley and other flours will make an acceptable bread to replace the heavier kind of coarse, wholewheat bread. If you are used to the light, white type of bread and crave for it, a blended flour with less rye is perhaps more suitable, or a special flour such as Trufree No. 1 (see p. 123).

Before going further, we need to have a look at the basics of good nutrition. A healthy body needs protein, fat, carbohydrate, fibre, water and essential vitamins, minerals and trace elements (micronutrients). All these come in foods, generally in a mixture rather than singly. The body has to digest food and use it for energy, movement, work, growth, repair and (sometimes) reproduction. Most of what we eat is broken down chemically by the digestive system and passed into the bloodstream to be carried to where it is needed in the body. Waste is passed out and so are waste liquids.

In the western world we enjoy a mixed diet made up of a wide variety of foods. This is to our advantage as we have the opportunity of taking in everything we need for our bodies to function and keep healthy.

GOOD SOURCES OF PROTEIN, FAT, CARBOHYDRATE AND FIBRE FOR A WHEAT-FREE DIET

Protein: Cheddar-type cheese, Parmesan cheese, lean back bacon; lean grilling, stewing or roasting beef; lean leg of lamb or pork; wheat-free corned beef; fish, eggs.

The body mainly uses protein for energy, growth and repair. Unfortunately it is not usually available on its own but is often combined with fat, as in meat.

Carbohydrate: Sweetcorn, maize flour, rice, special wheat-free muesli, raisins, sultanas, honey, potatoes, millet, rye, barley, bananas.

The highest carbohydrate food is sugar which is pure carbohydrate and not a good idea in large amounts.

Fat: Butter, wheat-free margarine, cream, full fat cheeses; walnuts, almonds, brazils; oils: sunflower, olive, safflower, corn and nut.

Fat may be saturated, polyunsaturated or monounsaturated, and eating some of all three kinds gives the best balance. Usually people eat too much saturated fat which can lead to health problems and overweight. Lard is highly saturated, as are butter and the fat on meat. Olive oil is largely monounsaturated. Cheese and corn, nut and seed oils are partly saturated and partly unsaturated. See the table at the end of this book (p. 124).

Fibre: Oats, oat bran, soya bran, rice bran, beans, root and leafy vegetables, sweetcorn, dried raw apricots and figs, or fresh fruit with pips and/or seeds.

As wheat bran is the most effective fibre for the digestive system, without it there is a risk that transit of food through the body will slow down too much. Other brans, such as oat, rice and soya, are not usually as effective as wheat bran. Plenty of fruit and vegetable fibre can help, as can drinking water (plain, not fizzy) throughout the day, and regular exercise.

MICRONUTRIENTS

The important vitamins and minerals in wheat are iron, zinc, thiamine (Vitamin B1), riboflavin (Vitamin B2), nicotinic acid (Vitamin B3) and Vitamin E. All these have to be put back into the diet when wheat is excluded. Even the outer covering of the wheat berries (wheat bran) contains phosphorus, iron, zinc, Vitamin B6, folic acid, pantothenic acid and biotin. Some people may need a wheat-free vitamin and mineral supplement to help them over the first days of the new diet. Choose one that is a good source of B-complex as well as the other vitamins and minerals, and make sure you choose a tablet that is wheat-free as usually there will be some kind of filler. When things settle down and your diet is balanced again you probably will not need any supplement.

You may not have considered before what micronutrients are for and which foods contain them. The table below lists important sources for someone on a wheat-free diet.

Table 1. Micronutrients and wheat-free sources.

Micronutrient and its purpose	Good wheat-free sources	Sources lost on a wheat-free diet
Vitamin A repair, protection from infection, eye and skin health, can help prevent cancer.	liver, fish oils, carrots, green vegetables.	wheatgerm, wheat bran, wheat breakfast cereals.
Vitamin B1 (thiamine) aids digestion, nerve health.	rye/barley/oats, wholegrains, brewer's yeast, meats.	wheat bran, wheatgerm, wheat breakfast cereals.
Vitamin B2 (riboflavin) cell formation, eye and skin health.	yeast, milk, eggs, green vegetables, liver, kidney.	wheatgerm.

Micronutrient and its purpose	Good wheat-free sources	Sources lost on a wheat-free diet
Vitamin B3 (niacin) prevention of severe skin disorders, cholesterol reduction, healthy heart.	eggs, wholegrains except wheat, milk, liver, kidneys, nuts, seafood, yeast.	wheat wholegrain.
Vitamin B5 (pantothenic acid) adrenal gland functioning, immune system.	dates, rye, barley, oats, brewer's yeast, eggs, mushrooms, liver, legumes, green vegetables, peanuts, milk, molasses.	wheat bran.
Vitamin B6 metabolism.	yeast, liver, rye, barley, oats, meat, green vegetables, nuts, fresh and dried fruits.	none.
Vitamin B12 iron metabolism, nerve condition, cell life.	liver, meat, eggs, fish.	none.
Folic acid prevents anaemia, neural tube defects.	eggs, liver, leafy green vegetables, milk, grains except wheat.	wheat.
Choline metabolism.	brewer's yeast, soya beans, egg yolk, legumes.	none.
Inositol detoxifier.	brewer's yeast, whole grains except wheat, meat, nuts, fruit.	wheat, wheat bran.

Micronutrient and its purpose	Good wheat-free sources	Sources lost on a wheat-free diet
Vitamin C anti-scurvy, healing of wounds, general health.	fresh fruit and vegetables especially citrus fruits and green peppers, new potatoes, UHT fortified milk.	none.
Vitamin D building healthy bones and teeth.	fish oils, eggs yolks, milk.	none.
Vitamin E protection of cells, aids healing process.	soya beans, sprouting seeds except wheat berries, dark green vegetables, eggs, nuts, vegetable oils except wheatgerm oil.	wheatgerm, wheatgerm oil, wheat-based cereals.
Vitamin F prostaglandins formation, healthy blood cholesterol levels.	sunflower, safflower and corn oils.	wheatgerm oil.
Biotin metabolism, growth.	brewer's yeast, egg yolks, liver, kidney, whole grains except wheat.	wheat wholegrain.
Calcium formation of bones, teeth, blood clotting, nerve and muscle control, heart condition.	milk, cheese, grains except wheat, fish, edible fish bones (as in canned salmon and sardines), dried apricots, spinach.	wheat flour, wheat bread, baked wheat products, i.e. cakes, biscuits, pastry.

NUTRITION FOR A WHEAT-FREE DIET

Micronutrient and its purpose	Good wheat-free sources	Sources lost on a wheat-free diet
Iodine formation of thyroid hormones, metabolic processes.	seafood.	none.
Iron red blood cell production, growth, stress control.	dark meat, poultry, cereals except wheat, seafood, molasses, liver.	wheatgerm, wheat bran, wholewheat flour, bread with wheatgerm, wheat.
Manganese sex hormone formation, memory, irritability.	cereals except wheat, green leafy vegetables, nuts, legumes.	wheat.
Magnesium cell function and enzyme systems, bone and tooth formation, heart and circulation.	green vegetables, cereals except wheat, honey, low fat soya flour, wheat-free muesli, almonds, brazils, wheat-free cocoa powder.	wheat, wheat bran, wheatgerm.
Phosphorus aids body processes.	eggs, meat, poultry, milk, grains except wheat, fish, legumes.	wheat.
Potassium heart and blood circulation, muscle function, energy, metabolism.	green vegetables, fresh fruit, dried fruit, nuts, seafood, sunflower seeds, legumes.	none.
Selenium cell life.	whole cereals except wheat, seafoods, milk, eggs, brewer's yeast.	wholewheat.

Micronutrient and its purpose	Good wheat-free sources	Sources lost on a wheat-free diet
Sodium essential to life, muscle contraction, normal cellular fluids.	table and cooking salt, milk, cheese, processed foods.	none.
Zinc metabolism, healing, digestion, gland function.	nuts, grains, legumes, oysters, seafoods, liver, meat.	wheat bran, wheat bran breakfast cereals.

Mineral Advantage of a Wheat-Free Diet
An advantage of a wheat-free diet is that by avoiding *wheat bran* you will have a better chance of absorbing zinc, iron and calcium. This is because wheat bran contains phytates which bind with these three important minerals during digestion, thus hindering their absorption.

BASIC BALANCE

People on a normal Western diet tend to eat too much fat, salt and sugar and not enough fresh fruit, vegetables or fibre. It is equally easy to eat badly on a wheat-free diet, for it allows you to make the same mistakes. To help you balance your diet properly, below is a list of *suggested* foods for one week. Small children will need less, growing teenagers more, women around what it suggests and men a little more.

Guide to amounts and kinds of food for one person (per week) on a wheat-free diet

Milk	3 pints (1.5 litres) skimmed milk
Eggs	6

Fats/oils	about 4 oz (110 g) polyunsaturated margarine and under 2 oz (50 g) butter
	4 oz (110 g) cheeses, preferably low fat
	total 9 fluid oz (250 ml) sunflower, safflower, corn, soya or olive oil (varied)
Vegetables	4 lb (2 kg) potatoes (fresh)
	3 oz (75 g) frozen peas
	2½ lb (1.25 kg) fresh green and other vegetables including salads
Meat (lean only) from	4½ oz (125 g) beef
	2 oz (50 g) liver
	2½ oz (65 g) lamb
	10 oz (280 g) poultry
	4 oz (110 g) bacon/ham without breadcrumb coating
	2½ oz (65 g) pork
	2 homemade sausages (see recipe p. 60) made with special wheat-free breadcrumbs
Fish	about 12 oz (350 g) oily and white fish, fresh and canned in oil or water (not sauce)
Sugar/jam/honey	no more than total 7 oz (200 g) = 1 oz (25 g) per day
Wheat-free pasta and flours/rice (cooked)	1 lb (500 g)
Fruit	over 2 lb (1 kg) fresh fruit
	2 oz (50 g) low sugar canned fruit
	8 oz (225 g) dried fruit including apricots
Nuts	1–2 oz (25–50g) plain nuts
Bread	3 small wheat-free loaves, scones and crispbreads to total 1½ lb (700 g) (see recipes)

Cereals	8 oz (225 g) oats/rice-based cereals/ barley/rye/millet flakes
	2 oz (50 g) rice bran/soya bran/oat bran
Cakes/buns/ pastries/ biscuits	about 8 oz (225 g) wheat-free
Pulses (peas, beans)	2 oz (50 g) dried weight
Beverages	2–3 oz (50–75 g), wheat-free
Other foods	9 oz (250 g), wheat-free

Each day try to eat at least one portion of a leafy green vegetable—spinach, cabbage, greens, kale, cos lettuce—and three pieces of fresh fruit. Allow two meals per day with high protein foods and vegetables. Make sure you eat enough carbohydrates from bread and cereals and try to keep your fat and salt intake low, and to eat plenty of fibre. The alternative is just the opposite, with a good deal of junk food—sugary, fatty, salty, processed food, sweets, chocolates. The result is bound to be poor health. Remember, good health is probably the most important feature of your life and what you eat can make a major contribution to achieving it. Good health is beyond price, and although a wheat-free diet is not the same as an ordinary diet, your own good health can be gained and maintained with knowledge, common sense and a little effort.

EMERGENCY WHEAT-FREE DIET

While you are getting things organised on the shopping and kitchen front, it may be helpful to use the following two-day plan for food. It will also help those who are not used to coping with a wheat-free diet and suddenly have to do so for a visitor. It does not involve any special foods and can be organised by shopping in a supermarket or at your local butcher, fishmonger, greengrocer and grocer.

Day 1   *Breakfast:*   cornflakes, milk, sugar
grilled back bacon and fresh tomatoes
fresh orange juice
NO BREAD, ROLLS or TOAST

Lunch: plain boiled or jacket potato
lettuce, tomato, cucumber, radish
salad
dressing: 2 teaspoons sunflower oil +
1 teaspoon wine vinegar
grated cheese
NO BREAD, ROLLS or TOAST
apple, pear or grapes

Dinner: grilled lean steak or lamb chops
boiled rice or boiled potatoes
carrots, spring greens or sprouts with
butter
NO GRAVY
NO BREAD, ROLLS or TOAST
fresh fruit salad

Day 2   *Breakfast:*   rolled oats, grated apple
almonds/hazelnuts, sultanas, milk and
sugar
scrambled egg, fried boiled potato
NO BREAD, ROLLS or TOAST

Lunch: cold boiled rice, chopped tomato,
cucumber, spring onion, grated carrot
mixed together, lettuce
dressing: 2 teaspoons sunflower oil and
1 teaspoon fresh lemon juice
sliced cold ham (without breadcrumb
coating) or cold beef, pork or plain
roast chicken (no stuffing)
NO BREAD, ROLLS or TOAST
banana

27

Dinner: fillet of cod, haddock or plaice baked in
              lemon juice (see Chapter 6)
              peas, carrots, boiled potatoes
              NO BREAD, ROLLS or TOAST
              plain stewed fruit with brown sugar
              (apple, rhubarb, etc.)

IMPORTANT: Do not serve any kind of bread, crispbread, biscuits, gravy or sauce. For seasoning use salt and freshly ground black pepper. Use sunflower oil and butter, fresh fruit and vegetables, fresh or frozen plain meat and fish.

STAPLES

It is a good idea always to have by you some cold, boiled rice and cold, boiled potato. They are invaluable carbohydrate foods and both can be fried, put into soups or salads cold, used for breakfast, lunch, supper and for lunchboxes. The potato can be mashed and used as a thickener. Don't keep for more than two days and store covered in the fridge. Buy rye and barley flours.

Instead of wheat flour, stock up with Trufree flour, a 100 per cent wheat-free blend of maize, rice, soya and potato flours with an added binder. The range includes flours suitable for all types of baking and the results are indistinguishable from wheat flour versions. Buy at chemists, health food shops or by mail. See p. 123 for details. If you have a craving for wheat this will probably satisfy it.

BREAKFAST

Breakfast, that most unpopular of meals, is important for the wheat-free dieter and gives a good start to the day. A small breakfast can comprise plain yoghurt and stewed or fresh fruit with a little honey or sugar, or there are wheat-free cereals such as cornflakes and oat porridge which have instructions on the packet. Serve with sugar and milk. Millet can also be used for porridge.

For a more substantial breakfast, any of the following can be used. Bacon and mushrooms; bacon, bubble and squeak (potato and greens, both precooked, fried in a little sunflower oil into a kind of savoury cake); scrambled egg and bacon; bacon, lightly fried precooked potato and a poached or fried egg; homemade fishcakes (mashed potato, cooked fish and a little parsley, dipped in wheat-free cornflour and beaten egg, fried in a little sunflower oil on both sides) served with grilled tomatoes; poached haddock with egg (also poached); cooked potato omelet with bacon. If wheat-free bread is available, serve it toasted with poached, scrambled or boiled egg. For a cold breakfast serve ham (without breadcrumb coating) and tomato. Avoid too much fat for hot breakfasts, grilling bacon (lean) rather than using the frying-pan. Wheat-free bread or toast, margarine and marmalade will fill the gap for dieters with a good appetite. (See also pancakes, chapter 11.)

CHAPTER 3

Basics for a Wheat-Free Diet

This chapter deals with basic ingredients and kitchen equipment required to follow a wheat-free diet. It also offers advice on avoiding contamination with wheat and on where to buy particular ingredients that may be new to you.

EQUIPMENT

You will need no specialised gadgets or kitchen equipment, but it is wise to keep, and mark in some way, a set of equipment just for wheat-free baking and cooking. There is a risk of contamination from wooden spoons, chopping boards, baking tins and sheets that have not been properly cleaned after wheat cooking and baking; also from the toaster (already discussed in chapter 1), the grill and worktops, storage containers and actual packets of wheat.

It is good kitchen policy to have a special apron or overall that is worn just for wheat-free work. Always wash your hands thoroughly before you start and clean under your fingernails.

Keep wheat flour well away from wheat-free ingredients which should preferably be kept in a cupboard on their own and *must* be kept in their own containers. Also store wheat-free bread in its own container and not with wheat bread. The same applies to cakes, biscuits, crispbreads and so on. A distinctive set of storage tins and jars is a good idea. Mark them clearly and use them all the time—it will make life easier.

Mark wooden spoons and wire racks by tying a piece of cotton to them. Scratch marks on baking tins with a file so that they can be identified. Instead of the toaster, use a clean grill pan and grid for making toast.

Always make a point of cleaning up well after you have been working in the kitchen as it helps to avoid accidental contamination with wheat. If you need to do both kinds of cooking and baking, do the wheat-free first as it doesn't matter if this contaminates the wheat activity.

Below is a complete list of basic kitchen equipment used for recipes in this book. Those items marked with an asterisk * are the ones you may need to keep separately, just for the wheat-free food.

KITCHEN EQUIPMENT

patty tins, cake papers
*1 lb loaf tin, 6″ long, 4″ wide at the top, 2¾″ deep
*baking sheet
*cake tin size 9″ (22.5 cm) diameter
*sponge tins 8″ (20 cm) diameter
*wooden spoons
measuring jug and measuring spoons
wire mesh sieve/strainer
colander
piping bag and nozzle for *éclairs* and *langues de chat*
bowls, basins

whisk
knives
ovenproof plate for tarts
spatula
saucepans—keep a set just
  for wheat-free cooking
kitchen scissors
liquidiser for soups and
  batters
heavy base frying pan (see
  saucepans)

garlic press
wok or large frying pan with
  sloping sides for stir/fry
roasting tin
*chopping board—if
  wooden
pie dishes
kebab skewers
food processor (only for
  sausages)
gravy separater

Shopping, preparation, storage and eating all take on a new meaning when a strict special diet is involved. To help you with choice of foods (often a worry) the following table gives a long basic list of foods and ingredients, showing you at a glance which ones are wheat-free, which are not and which may or may not be wheat-free according to the brand used.

Notes on the following table: Foods marked with ● can be purchased at health food shops. Any food marked with a question mark requires careful choice of brand. Check ingredients before using.

Table 2.   Guide to wheat-free foods and those to be avoided.

Food	Wheat-free YES/NO √ ✕	? Wheat-free depending on brand	Uses and comments
arrowroot	√		For thickening stews, gravies, sauces, casseroles, etc., expensive.
baby foods		?	Ask at your chemists for safe brands.

Food	Wheat-free YES/NO ✓ ✗	? Wheat-free depending on brand	Uses and comments
bacon/ham	✓		Use ham without breadcrumb coating.
baked beans		?	Tomato sauce often contains wheat.
barley • barley flakes • barley meal • pot barley pearl barley	 ✓ ✓ ✓ ✓		 For muesli and granola. For baking. For stews, casseroles. For barley water, stews, casseroles.
batter mixes	✗		
bedtime drinks		?	
biscuits	✗		
black treacle	✓		
blancmange		?	
bread/rolls/ crispbreads	✗		
burgers	✗		
buckwheat • buckwheat flour • buckwheat flakes	 ✓ ✓		Not a kind of wheat but a member of the rhubarb family. For pancakes. For muesli.
butter	✓		
cakes/cake decorations	✗		
chocolate		?	
cookies	✗		

Food	Wheat-free YES/NO ✓ ✗	? Wheat-free depending on brand	Uses and comments
cereals (breakfast)		?	Avoid Puffed and Shredded Wheat, Wheat Flakes, All-Bran and other wheat-based cereals and muesli mixes.
cheese, plain spreads	✓	?	
chutney		?	
cream, dairy imitation	✓ ✗		

coffee, pure
  from vending
  machines
	✓
	✗
			Carry your own with you.

custard, canned
  packet mix
  powder
		?
		?
		?	

dumplings	✗		
desserts		?	
eggs	✓		Avoid Scotch egg, mayonnaise, quiche with pastry.

fish, plain, fresh
  canned in sauce
  canned in oil
  frozen, plain
  in batter
  in crumb
    coating
  in breadcrumbs
  dipped in flour
	✓
	✗
	✓
	✓
	✗
	✗
	
	✗
	✗		

flour/flour products
  wheat
  wheat berries/
    grains
  wheatmeal
	✗
	✗
	
	✗		

BASICS FOR A WHEAT-FREE DIET

Food	Wheat-free YES/NO ✓ ✗	? Wheat-free depending on brand	Uses and comments
wholewheat	✗		Instead use rye,
wheat flour	✗		barley, oats, millet,
wheat starch	✗		potato, rice, maize.
durum wheat	✗		
semolina	✗		
couscous	✗		
wheatgerm	✗		
cracked wheat	✗		
kibbled wheat	✗		
pourgouri	✗		
burghul	✗		
bulghar wheat	✗		
wheat bran	✗		
granary flour	✗		
wheat flakes	✗		
rusk	✗		
fruit, fresh	✓		
canned	✓		
pie fillings	✗		
pure juices	✓		
drinks		?	
gelatine	✓		For setting jellies.
glacé cherries	✓		Rinse well before using.
golden syrup	✓		
herbs, plain fresh/ dried	✓		
ice cream		?	
meat/poultry, fresh, plain	✓		
frozen, plain	✓		
in crumbs	✗		
in batter	✗		
dipped in flour	✗		
in pies		?	
in rissoles		?	
canned		?	Avoid corned beef, luncheon meats.
sauces		?	
with stuffing	✗		

Food	Wheat-free YES/NO ✓ ✗	? Wheat-free depending on brand	Uses and comments
honey, pure honey spreads	✓	?	
lentils	✓		
maize/sweetcorn • maize meal	✓ ✓		Often called *masa harina*, use for tortillas, tacos, cornbread.
• hominy grits	✓		Coarsely ground for porridge.
cornflour		?	Look for 'pure maize' on label, for white sauce, custard, thickening gravies, stews, casseroles.
marmalade	✓		
mayonnaise		?	
milk, plain drinks puddings	✓	? ?	
• millet	✓		
MSG (monosodium glutamate)		?	Can be made from wheat starch.
mustard, English	✗		Usually contains wheat by tradition.
French	✓		Genuine French brands are wheat-free.
nuts/seeds, plain coated	✓	?	
oats rolled oats	✓		For muesli, porridge, baking.
jumbo oats	✓		For muesli.
wholegrain oats	✓		Boil as for pulses.
pinhead oatmeal	✓		For stews, casseroles.
oatbran	✓		For baking.
oatgerm	✓		For baking.

BASICS FOR A WHEAT-FREE DIET

Food	Wheat-free YES/NO ✓ ✗	? Wheat-free depending on brand	Uses and comments
oils			
sunflower	✓		
safflower	✓		
corn	✓		
soya	✓		
peanut/ groundnut	✓		
olive	✓		
wheatgerm	✗		Avoid margarine with wheatgerm oil.
grapeseed	✓		
walnut	✓		
sesame	✓		
pancakes	✗		
pasta	✗		
pastry	✗		
pâté/paste		?	
peel	✓		Rinse well before using.
pepper			
black, whole peppercorns	✓		
white, ground		?	Sometimes 'stretched' with wheat flour for catering.
pizza	✗		
rice, plain	✓		
ground	✓		
flour	✓		
wild rice	✓		Not a true rice.
rye			
● flakes	✓		For muesli.
● flour	✓		For baking.
● meal	✓		For baking.
salad dressings		?	

Food	Wheat-free YES/NO √ ×	? Wheat-free depending on brand	Uses and comments
salt	√		
sausages		?	Usually include rusk.
sauces		?	Often thickened with wheat.
soya			
● flour	√		
● bran	√		
sauce		?	Look for Tamari, mixture of soya/rice.
● beans	√		
soups		?	
spreads		?	
stock/gravy			Avoid brands with MSG.
mixes		?	
cubes		?	
granules		?	
paste		?	
stuffing/stuffing mixes	×		Usually made with breadcrumbs.
suet		?	Often rolled in wheat flour.
tea, plain loose	√		
plain, teabags	√		
herbal teabags/ mixtures		?	Check ingredients labels.
tomato purée	√		
TVP (textured vegetable protein)		?	
vegetables, plain	√		
fresh	√		
frozen		?	
canned		?	
in batter	×		
in sauce		?	

Food	Wheat-free YES/NO √ ×	? Wheat-free depending on brand	Uses and comments
vinegar	√		
yeast, pure	√		
yeast extract	√		
yoghurt		?	Plain, unflavoured brands are safest.

FITTING IN WITH FAMILY AND FRIENDS

The person who lives alone is at an advantage when following a wheat-free diet. For others, in a family situation, it can be more difficult. Does everybody eat the same food or should there be two separate kinds of food, one for the special dieter and another for the rest of the family? Should the whole family be 'punished' with wheat-free food? The answer is that there will be times when everyone can eat the same food and other times where the wheat-free dieter has to eat a separate meal, albeit at the same table. This can be difficult for the dieter, the rest of the family and the cook. It is very easy to make special dieters feel they are being a nuisance. However, with understanding, planning and empathy a great deal can be achieved.

EATING OUT

Eating out can be fraught with difficulties. Even a top chef is unlikely to know anything about a wheat-free diet. The best advice is to choose dishes you know will be wheat-free. Unfortunately, accidental contamination from equipment and other food is a risk that has to be taken. Here is an eating out plan that never fails for a wheat-free diet.

Starter: avoid soup and anything with mayonnaise, pâtés, terrines, fish cocktails. Choose melon or parma ham and melon.

Main course: plain grilled steak or fish, plain omelette, plain vegetables with butter, NO gravy, sauce or dressing. Use freshly ground black pepper.

Sweet: fresh, plain fruit and dairy cream—NO ice cream, puddings, pies, desserts, ice cream wafers.

Coffee: freshly ground coffee or tea with milk.

All sherry, wine, champagne, whisky, brandy are suitable —any drink not made from wheat.

For children eating out, the same menu applies, minus the alcohol. Fresh fruit juice, mineral water or plain milk can usually be ordered.

If at all possible, take your own packed meal rather than eat out. See Chapter 12 for ideas and advice on this worry-free solution.

CHAPTER 4

Soups and Starters

SOUPS

As many kinds of soup contain a thickener (usually wheat flour), it is comforting to know there is a selection which does not need thickening at all, being naturally the correct consistency. These also have the advantage of being filling—an important feature when wheat has been removed from the diet—and can be eaten without the traditional accompaniment of wheat bread or rolls. Some of them will be familiar, which helps to reassure the dieter that not everything previously enjoyed needs to be avoided on the new regime.

41

Stock

You will need to take care with your selection of stock. Most commercial stocks contain wheat as a binder/thickener or MSG (monosodium glutamate) the flavour enhancer which is often made from wheat starch. Find a supply of wheat-free soy sauce and keep more than one bottle in the store cupboard (a health food shop or delicatessen is the most likely source). Look for the label 'wheat-free' on the front of the bottle as well as checking the ingredients list. If you cannot find a suitable brand it is possible to make your own (see Chapter 11 for meat and vegetable stock).

When making hot soups, avoid letting them boil. This undoubtedly leads to better flavour and colour. Good quality fresh ingredients instead of leftovers will also help.

Mushroom Soup (serves 2)

Probably the quickest and tastiest soup there is. Use either white button mushrooms or field mushrooms. White ones make a pale-coloured soup; the field variety make a dark, greyish brown soup.

½ medium onion, sliced
2 teaspoons sunflower oil
2 oz (50 g) mushrooms,
    sliced
Under ½ pint (300 ml)
    water

2 teaspoons wheat-free soy
    sauce or stock of your
    choice
Salt and freshly ground
    black pepper

Method: Use a small pan to fry the onion gently in the oil for four to five minutes, without letting it brown. Put the raw mushrooms into the blender. Add the cooked onion, the water and stock. Blend and pour into the pan. Bring to the boil then simmer for another four to five minutes. Taste and season. Serve hot.

Take care with your stock—it must be wheat-free.

Lentil Soup (serves 2)

This cheerful soup is extra filling and good winter fare. It also stands being reheated well. The dried lentils come in various colours: browns, greens and red. The latter is the most attractive but they all produce a good flavoured soup. It is not absolutely essential to soak them overnight. You can use unsoaked lentils but they will need extra water added and will take longer to cook. Some lentils have a peppery taste and do not require black pepper seasoning.

2½ oz (75 g) lentils
1 medium onion, chopped
1 small potato, sliced
1 tablespoon sunflower oil
½ pint (300 ml) water

2–3 teaspoons wheat-free soy sauce or stock of your choice
Salt and freshly ground pepper (optional)

Method: Put the lentils in a wire sieve and wash under the cold tap, removing any grit. Soak overnight in a bowl of water, allowing them to swell. The following day, fry the onion in the oil, using a medium-sized pan. Add the stock, water, strained, soaked lentils, potato and a pinch of salt. Bring to the boil then simmer for about 40–45 minutes topping up with more water if required. Take off the heat and leave to cool for a few minutes. Liquidise to make a smooth, creamy soup. Season to taste and serve.

Take care with your stock—it must be wheat-free.

Tomato and Basil Soup (serves 2)

½ medium onion, chopped
2 teaspoons olive oil
1 small can peeled tomatoes in tomato juice
½ pint (300 ml) water
¼ teaspoon sugar

2 teaspoons wheat-free soy sauce or stock of your choice
Salt and freshly ground black pepper to taste
4 leaves freshly chopped basil

Method: Put the onion into a medium-sized pan with the oil and stir/fry for about five minutes. Spoon the tomatoes/

juice and half the water into the liquidiser. Add the cooked onion and blend. Pour back into the pan and heat through, adding more water and stock. Taste and add the basil, sugar and seasoning. Serve hot.

If fresh basil is not available, use ½ level teaspoon dried basil.

Take care with the stock—it must be wheat-free.

Tomato Soup
Make as for Tomato and Basil Soup but substitute parsley for the basil.

Pea Soup (serves 2)

½ medium onion, chopped
2 teaspoons sunflower oil
Less than ½ pint (300 ml) water
6 oz (175 g) frozen peas

2 teaspoons wheat-free soy sauce or stock of your choice
Salt and freshly ground black pepper

Method: Fry the onion in the oil until transparent but do not let it brown. Pour in half the water, put in the peas and stock. Bring to the boil, slowly. Simmer for five or six minutes and add the remaining water. Pour into the liquidiser and blend. Reheat, season to taste and serve hot.

Take care with the stock—it must be wheat-free.

Vegetable Soups
The variety of vegetables available all year round does not seem to vary much. This is sad as it encourages the same vegetable soup recipe to be used, month in, month out. Take advantage of gluts of cheap vegetables or those in their true seasons; then you will enjoy variety in flavour, colour and texture.

The method is the same for all vegetable soups.

Method for Vegetable Soups

Use a large saucepan to fry the onion in the oil. Add the rest of the vegetable selection and about ⅔ of the water. Put in the stock, bring to the boil, then simmer for about 15–20 minutes with the lid on. Remove from heat, add any remaining water and spoon/pour into the liquidiser. Blend and pour back into the pan. Heat through, season to taste and serve hot with the appropriate garnish.

Spring Vegetable Soup (serves 2)

½ medium onion, sliced
Green from 2 large spinach
  leaves (or equivalent
  small leaves)
4 cauliflower florets,
  chopped
1 small carrot, sliced thinly
1 small leek, sliced
½ pint (300 ml) water

2 teaspoons wheat-free soy
  sauce or suitable stock of
  your choice
Salt and freshly ground
  black pepper
1 heaped teaspoon freshly
  chopped parsley for
  garnish

Method: See above. Take care with the stock—it must be wheat-free.

Chicken Soup (serves 2)

2 raw chicken drumsticks
½ pint (300 ml) water
1 small carrot, sliced thinly
1 onion, sliced
½ stick celery, chopped
1 small tomato, halved
Salt and black pepper
½ bay leaf

3 teaspoons wheat-free soy
  sauce or stock of your
  choice
½ teaspoon finely grated
  lemon rind
2 heaped teaspoons freshly
  chopped parsley

Method: Use a medium-sized pan and put in the chicken and water. Bring to the boil and skin off any scum that forms. Put in the carrot, onion, celery, tomato, black pepper and bay leaf. Bring back to the boil then simmer for

45 minutes. Strain off the liquid into a bowl, using a fine sieve and reserving the chicken. Discard the skin and bones. Chop the flesh into small pieces and add to the liquid in the pan. Add the stock, lemon rind and parsley and reheat. Season to taste and serve hot.

A tablespoon of cooked rice can be added before serving.

Take care with the stock—it must be wheat-free.

Cold Cucumber Soup (serves 2)

Use cucumber, yoghurt and milk chilled from the fridge.

¾ small carton plain yoghurt (about 4 oz/100 g)
½ medium cucumber
2 fresh mint leaves, chopped finely

Freshly ground black pepper to season
6 slices cucumber for garnish
Salt to taste

Method: Blend the cucumber, yoghurt and a grind of pepper in a liquidiser. Pour into a basin. Stir in the chopped mint, taste and season. Spoon in a little cold milk if you judge the soup to be too thick. Stir well and pour into two soup bowls. Float three slices of cucumber on each one and serve immediately.

This is a useful summer soup as it requires no thickening and no stock. If preferred, garnish each bowl with a mint leaf instead of the cucumber.

STARTERS

These are appetisers to get the appetite going and encourage the flow of digestive juices. Emphasis is on colour, taste and presentation. Fruit is an easy choice for the wheat-free dieter and it is not too filling. Protein in the form of fish, meat or a pâté can be served if the portion is small. Traditionally bread in some form is served with protein. See Chapter 10 for special wheat-free recipes.

Dips

For the wheat-free dieter, the following nibbles of *raw* vegetables are always safe:

Cauliflower florets	Small crisp lettuce leaves
Sticks of fennel	(e.g. little gem)
Carrot sticks	Strips of red, green or
Cucumber sticks	yellow pepper
Tomato wedges	Radishes
Trimmed spring onions	Small sticks of celery

Serve arranged neatly on a plate with a small dipping dish of wheat-free mayonnaise or vinaigrette (see Chapter 7).

Commercial mayonnaise is frequently not wheat-free. If you are using this kind instead of homemade, study the ingredients list carefully.

Avocado and Orange

For each person you will need ½ a ripe medium-sized avocado and ½ an orange. Peel and stone the avocado and cut into slices longways. Arrange on a plate in a fan shape. Peel the orange and cut out clean segments using a sharp knife. Arrange between the avocado slices. To avoid discolouration, immediately spoon over a little oil and vinegar dressing—1 part sunflower oil to 2 parts wine vinegar and a little sugar to taste. Lastly, grind a little black pepper over the fruit and serve with a small knife and fork.

Avocado and Raspberry Sauce

A very simple but stylish and colourful starter. For each person you will need ½ a ripe avocado and a few fresh or frozen raspberries—about 1 heaped tablespoon. First make the sauce. Put the raspberries into a liquidiser with one tablespoon cold water and ½ teaspoon castor sugar.

Blend. Peel and stone the avocado, cut into long thin slices and lay them slightly overlapping on a plate. Pour the raspberry dressing carefully around the avocado and serve immediately before it discolours. Serve with a knife and fork. The sauce should be slightly tart. A good last-minute dish to serve at a dinner party.

Smoked Salmon with Chives and Lemon

For each person you will need 1½ (40 g)–2 oz (50 g) thinly sliced smoked salmon. Lay on a plate, sprinkle with a heaped teaspoon finely chopped fresh chives and squeeze over a little fresh lemon juice. Garnish with lemon slices. Serve with brown wheat-free bread and butter. See Chapter 10 for recipe.

Parma Ham with Fruit

For each person you will need 2 thin slices of Parma ham (prosciutto) and either 2 ripe kiwi fruits or ¼ medium-sized ripe melon, pips removed. Peel and cut whichever fruit you have chosen into thin slices. Arrange on a plate and cover with the ham. Serve with a knife and fork. A grind of black pepper can be used as a garnish.

Pâtés

Pâtés can be a secret source of wheat as either wheat flour or wheat bread/rusk may be used as a thickener. MSG is used in many commercial pâtés and this could well be made from wheat starch. It is important to make this kind of food at home and so avoid problems. Use as a starter, a small snack or in sandwiches as a tasty filling.

Nut Pâté

Pâtés need not be made from liver. Here's a vegetarian one made from almonds or cashews, which is just as tasty.

1 tablespoon sunflower oil
1 spring onion, finely
 chopped
½ clove garlic
1 oz (25 g) ground rice or
 rice flour
6 tablespoons water
1 pinch nutmeg

2 oz (50 g) finely ground
 almonds or cashews
1 teaspoon tomato purée
1 heaped teaspoon freshly
 chopped parsley
Freshly ground black pepper
 to taste

Method: Fry the onion gently in the oil for about four minutes, while you stir from time to time. Crush in the garlic and continue to cook/stir for a few more seconds. Put in the rice and stir until it has absorbed all the oil. Lower the heat and cook gently while stirring for another minute. Pour in the water, slowly; stir well to avoid lumps. When you have a stiff paste add the nuts, spice, purée, parsley and seasoning. Mix well and turn out into a small dish. Serve hot or leave until cold and serve from the fridge. Eat within two days. Good as a sandwich filling. If serving hot, brown wheat-free toast (see Chapter 10) makes a good accompaniment.

CHAPTER 5

Main Meals With Meat and Accompaniments

HOT VEGETABLES AND ACCOMPANIMENTS

Potatoes

This versatile staple can be boiled, fried, roasted, steamed, mashed or baked. It is especially useful for a wheat-free diet as it is cheap and a good source of carbohydrate. However, being bland-tasting and fairly dry, potatoes lend themselves to being eaten with a large amount of fat. This should be avoided for health reasons. Probably the fattiest forms of potato are the roast potato allowed to cook swimming in fat, and the deep-fried chip. Both these nutritional disasters can be avoided.

Healthy Chips

Peel old potatoes and cut into chips. Spread in a large roasting tin and spoon in 1 teaspoon (yes, teaspoon) of sunflower oil per medium potato. Turn the chips over by hand to coat with the oil. Wipe your hands on kitchen paper and put the chips into a preheated oven, Gas 8/

230°C/450°F, on the top shelf for about 25 minutes. They will be crisp and golden. Serve immediately.

Roast Potatoes
Make in the same way as Healthy Chips but cut the potatoes into chunks.

Mashed Potatoes
Boil sliced, old potatoes in water for up to 20 minutes. Strain in a colander and put back into the pan. Mash and add salt and freshly ground pepper to taste, a pinch or two of nutmeg, a little milk and a knob of butter or wheat-free margarine. Beat with a wooden spoon.

Jacket Potatoes
Scrub old potatoes, cutting out any scars. Prick all over with a fork and bake in the oven at the top, either quickly or slowly depending upon what else you have in the oven. Gas 7/220°C/425°F for an hour or Gas 4/180°C/350°F for one-and-a-half hours. Encourage people to eat the skins and serve split with a knob (not lashings!) of butter or wheat-free margarine.

Rice
This has to be boiled in a generous amount of water. Unless you are buying loose rice, instructions will be on the packet. A guide for loose rice is about 40 minutes for brown rice and 20 to 30 minutes for white, depending on the variety. Drain in a colander. To reheat cooked rice, put in a fine mesh sieve and steam over a pan of boiling water for about eight minutes, covered.

Greens
Do please eat greens of some kind every day, and cook them so that the maximum nutrient value is obtained. They

need water but don't need to drown in it. Curly kale takes the longest to cook—up to 35 minutes for the dark green leaves; spring greens, sprout tops, sprouts and firm cabbage take about 25–30 minutes or less if they are young. Spinach requires only a little water and much less cooking. Drain well in a colander, pressing the leaves with the back of a large spoon. Young leaves will take 5–8 minutes, old leaves up to 12 minutes or so. All greens cook best with the lid on, moved over slightly to let out the steam. Always take care to drain well in a colander and serve immediately they are cooked. (The straining liquid can be used for gravy).

Root Vegetables
Eat carrots often—several times a week. Simmer in boiling water for up to 25 minutes if they are old or ten minutes if they are young. Slice or cut into long pieces before you cook them. For the last five minutes of cooking add frozen peas to the pan. Bring back to the boil and finish cooking the two vegetables together. A good mixture, colourful and usually popular with children who enjoy their sweet taste.

Parsnips are best roasted like potatoes. Cut into quarters and bake at the top of the oven. Again, this is a sweet vegetable. It can also be boiled and mashed as for mashed potato, without the nutmeg.

Swede is best boiled and mashed with a knob of wheat-free margarine and served to taste with salt and freshly ground black pepper. Try swede and potato cooked together and then mashed. They will take about 15–20 minutes if cut into small pieces.

Turnips should be cooked as for swede.

Beans
Green beans, string beans, stick beans, French beans and runner beans should be topped and tailed, cut into short

52

lengths and boiled for about eight minutes for young beans and up to 20–25 minutes for older beans. Runner beans will need the strings either side cutting off and they should be sliced through the little bean seeds inside, when they are cut up. A diagonal cut is best. Young string beans only need topping and can be cooked whole.

Dried beans need soaking overnight in plenty of water. Drain and cook in plenty of boiling water. Cook at a full rolling boil for the first ten minutes and then simmer. Beans already cooked and canned are a timesaver, but apart from genuine French brands canned in water, they usually come in a slightly thickened liquid. Check labels carefully before buying and using. Health food shops carry a wide variety of dried beans.

Broad beans need to be shelled and, if they are old, cooked for up to 25 minutes in boiling water. Younger, smaller beans will need 15–20 minutes.

Broccoli, Cauliflower, Purple Sprouting
Cut into florets and cook in a little boiling water for 8–15 minutes until tender but still quite crisp. Older sprouting may need up to 25 minutes.

Leeks
Trim and slice lengthways, washing well between the layers to get rid of any earth or grit. Young leeks will need boiling in water for about ten minutes; older leeks may require up to 25 minutes. Drain in the same way as spinach. Good served with wheat-free white sauce (see Chapter 7).

Beetroot
Cook whole, without cutting the root or skin, in plenty of boiling water. Old beetroot will need up to an hour if large. Young beet will probably only need 30 minutes. Drain and allow to cool. Peel off the skin, trim off the

root and top and cut into slices. Eat within two days of cooking.

Salads
These can be served as starters, between courses or as an accompaniment to plain cooked meat or fish—grilled, roast or baked. A salad every day is a sensible habit in terms of good nutrition, so variety is all-important.

Crisp Green Salad
In a bowl mix iceberg, little gem and watercress or cress. Dress with vinaigrette (see Chapter 7). Add slices of cucumber and spring onions or snipped chives. Season with salt and freshly ground black pepper to taste.

Green Salad with Garlic
Make in the same way as for green salad, but before you put the lettuce into the bowl, pour in a little of the dressing and use the cut edge of half a clove of garlic to rub all over the base and sides. This gives a delicate, as opposed to robust, flavour of garlic to the salad. Season with salt and freshly ground black pepper to taste.

Red Salad
In a bowl mix grated raw beetroot and carrot. Add chopped fresh tomatoes and dress with vinaigrette. Add a little finely chopped red onion and thin slices of red pepper for variation. Season with freshly ground black pepper to taste and dress with vinaigrette (see Chapter 7).

Winter Salad
In a bowl mix finely shredded, crisp white cabbage, chopped raw cauliflower, finely grated carrot and chopped celery. Add finely chopped onion and dress with a lemon vinaigrette (see Chapter 7). Season with freshly ground

black pepper to taste. Raw Brussels sprouts can be used instead of the cabbage.

Bean Salad
In a bowl, sprinkle cooked green beans with a little finely chopped onion. Dress with vinaigrette and season to taste with salt and freshly ground black pepper.

Pastas
As wheat or semolina pasta is off the menu, you will need to find a wheat-free type. Try your health food shop for alternative grain pastas or similar. Check labels carefully before buying and using.

Pancake flour blend (p. 108) will make a special kind of wheat-free pasta in five minutes. It doesn't require boiling in water and so is easy (if different) to make, using a liquidiser and frying pan.

Wheat-Free Pasta
Use pancake flour ingredients. Omit sugar; use water instead of milk. Put into a liquidiser; blend to make a thin, smooth batter. Using kitchen paper, lightly grease a non-stick frying pan with sunflower oil. Put over a high heat and when the pan is hot, pour in one third of the batter, tilting the pan to cover the base. Cook for only 30–40 seconds, then loosen with a spatula and turn over to cook for a few seconds on the other side. Don't cook too long until crisp (like a pancake); it should be pale in colour and soft. Keep on a warmed plate in the oven while you cook the other two amounts of batter. Stack them on a chopping board and cut into strips using a sharp knife.

Always have your sauce ready before you make this pasta—in other words, cook it last.

Crispy Noodles

Make as for pasta (above) but finish by frying the strips in a little hot sunflower oil. Serve immediately with Chinese food. (See this Chapter and Chapter 6. Chapter 7 has a sweet and sour sauce recipe for this kind of food.)

Stir/Fry Vegetables (serves 1)

This is a very useful method of cooking a variety of vegetables at once, as only one pan is required. Gravy can be made at the end of the cooking process by adding wheat-free thickener, water and wheat-free soy sauce to the juices. You will need a large pan with sloping sides or a wok (available from kitchen shops).

The vegetables should be shredded or sliced thinly. Always start with onion and then put in the remaining vegetables in order of hardness. Root vegetables such as carrots and potatoes first, then semi-hard such as celery, pepper, peas, beans and leafy vegetables, and lastly the soft ones such as mushrooms, cucumber, bean sprouts and tomatoes.

Avoid too many different vegetables at once as a smaller combination of just three or four is tastier. First put in a finely chopped onion and a tablespoon of sunflower oil. Fry gently for a few seconds just to get it started, then put in any hard vegetables such as thin carrot slices. Add a little water and turn the vegetables over with a large spoon while you cook them. After three or four minutes put in the semi-hard vegetables such as shredded cabbage.

Continue to stir and turn them over, adding a little more water just to stop them sticking (the juices will run out as they soften). After about three minutes put in the soft vegetables and cook for just another minute. Mix 2 table-spoons of water with 1 heaped teaspoon maize flour (wheat-free cornflour) and 1–2 teaspoons wheat-free soy sauce. Pour onto the middle of the pan. Cook for another

minute and the dish is ready—vegetables and a rich gravy.
Here are some suggestions for vegetable mixtures:

1 Spring onion, potatoes, carrots, spinach, mushrooms.
2 Spring onion, carrots, peas, green beans, spring greens
   (good with grilled steak).
3 Spring onion, potatoes, peas, tomato (good with liver).
4 Spring onion, carrots, celery, mushrooms, broccoli.
5 ¼ red onion, carrots, peas, cabbage.
6 Spring onion, carrots, celery, peppers, bean sprouts.

Ideal for serving with plain grilled fish or meat; also good as
a starter in winter. If using potato in the mixture of
vegetables, you may find that the gravy thickens naturally
and you won't need the maize flour.

PLAIN ROASTS

Forget roasting joints of meat like islands in a sea of fat.
Instead, roast in a roasting tin on a grid with two tablespoons of sunflower oil poured over the meat. Roast
potatoes and parsnips separately at the top of the oven (see
pp. 51, 52). The advantage of a roast joint or poultry is that
one hot meal can be taken off, leaving enough for one or
two cold meals. Here is a guide to roasting plain joints and
poultry.

To seal the meat or bird, prepare and put in the oven on a
high heat, Gas 8/230°C/450°F for about ten minutes, then
turn down the heat to Gas 5/190°C/275°F for whatever
cooking time is left. Calculate how long to cook meat and
poultry in the following way:

Beef: (rare) 15 minutes per lb (500 g) weight plus 15
           minutes over.
Beef: (well done) 20 minutes per lb (500 g) plus 20
           minutes over.
Chicken: 20 minutes per lb (500 g) plus 20 minutes
           over.

Lamb: 20 minutes per lb (500 g) plus 20 minutes over (or less if the meat has a bone running through it).

Pork: 35 minutes per lb (500 g) plus 35 minutes over. Pork must *never* be served undercooked.

Stuffings: Do not stuff a joint or bird unless you use a wheat-free stuffing (see Chapter 11 for details).

MEAT DISHES

Shepherd's Pie (3–4 servings)
This freezes well and can be made in individual portions for later use. Usually this kind of dish is thickened with wheat flour so it is worth making at home. Take care with your thickener and stock and use fresh potato, not instant.

1 tablespoon sunflower or olive oil
1 medium onion, chopped
12 oz (450 g) fresh, lean minced beef or lamb
2 medium mushrooms, chopped
½ clove garlic, crushed
1 medium carrot, finely grated
1 heaped tablespoon freshly chopped parsley
Knob of wheat-free margarine

1 teaspoon tomato purée
3 good pinches dried thyme or 1 teaspoon fresh leaves
3 teaspoons wheat-free soy sauce
1 heaped teaspoon maize flour (wheat-free cornflour)
3 medium potatoes, boiled
Little milk
Pinch nutmeg
Salt or freshly ground black pepper to taste

Method: Fry the onion gently in the oil for 4 minutes, using an ovenproof casserole. Put in the meat and stir/fry, turning it over until the colour turns to greyish brown. Add the mushrooms, garlic, carrot, purée, herbs and stock. Pour in enough water to almost cover the meat and bring to the boil. Simmer on a lower heat for about 20 minutes, giving it a stir from time to time. Mix the maize flour in a cup with

58

three teaspoons cold water. Bring the meat mixture to the boil again and stir in the thickening. Season to taste and keep warm while you make the topping.

Mash the potatoes with the margarine, a little milk and the nutmeg. Season to taste and spoon over the meat mixture. Flatten with a knife then fork it up to give it a texture. Make a hole in the centre to let out the steam and bake at Gas 5/190°C/375°F near the top of the oven for about 20 minutes, when the top will be crisp and browning. Serve hot with one or two green vegetables and/or grilled tomatoes.

If making individual pies, spoon the cooked meat mixture into appropriate containers and cover with the mashed potato. Allow to grow cold before freezing. To reheat, allow first to thaw completely then proceed as above.

Beefburgers (serves 2)

4 oz (100 g) extra lean minced beef

¼ medium onion, finely chopped

2 teaspoons wheat-free soy sauce

½ slice wheat-free bread (see Chapter 10) made into crumbs

½ egg, beaten

Small pinch dried mixed herbs

Freshly ground black pepper

Pinch salt

Maize flour for coating

Sunflower oil for shallow frying

Method: Except for the maize flour and oil, mix all ingredients in a basin. Shape into two round, flat burgers. Put a little maize flour on a plate and coat them all over. Fry in a little hot oil for two to three minutes. Turn over with a spatula and cook a further two to three minutes on the other side. Serve immediately. Good with healthy chips (see p. 50), peas and carrots. See Chapter 7 for gravy.

Wheat-Free Beef Sausages (makes 10)
Some to eat immediately and some to freeze. The apple
helps to bind the sausages.

8 oz (250 g) sirloin steak
trimmed of fat
2 slices wheat-free bread
(see Chapter 10)
1 eating apple
1 pinch dried thyme
1 pinch dried sage
2 pinches allspice
3 pinches salt
3 grinds black pepper

½ teaspoon made wheat-
free French mustard
1 tablespoon wheat-free soy
sauce
1 level teaspoon tomato
purée
Maize flour (wheat-free
cornflour) for coating
Sunflower oil for frying

Method: Cut the steak into small pieces. Finely grate the
apple including skin. Put the steak, wheat-free bread,
grated apple, herbs, spices, mustard, wheat-free soy sauce,
and purée into a food processor. Run the machine until you
have a coarse paste. Shape by hand into sausages and roll in
maize flour to coat. Fry in shallow oil for three minutes,
then turn over and fry another four minutes. Serve hot
with grilled tomatoes or heated canned plum tomatoes in
juice.

These sausages can also be made without a food processor. Put the steak through a fine mincer. Make the
bread into crumbs in a coffee grinder. Mix all sausage
ingredients together by hand to a coarse paste. Proceed as
above.

Sweet and Sour Pork
Take a slice or two of cold pork off a plain roasted joint and
cut into strips. Dip in maize flour (wheat-free cornflour)
and fry in a little sunflower oil. Serve with plain boiled rice
and stir/fry vegetables (see p. 56) and brown sweet and
sour sauce (see p. 76).

Gammon and Apricot Pie (serves 1)

This rather festive main meal can be used at Christmas when the rest of the family will be having turkey with wheat bread stuffing, wheat bread in the sausages, wheat bread sauce and wheat flour in the gravy! Do remember to soak the apricots the night before.

1 thick trimmed gammon rasher/steak	Wheat-free gravy (see Chapter 7)
6 dried apricot halves	Salt and freshly ground black pepper
1 teaspoon sultanas	
2 medium potatoes, sliced	

Method: Soak the apricots in water overnight. Put the rasher in a frying pan and brown lightly on both sides, turning over once. Put into an ovenproof pie dish. Drain the apricots and spread over the gammon with the sultanas. Pour a little wheat-free gravy over and season to taste. Top neatly with the potato slices. Cover with a piece of greaseproof paper and bake at Gas 6/200°C/400°F for about an hour. Serve hot with sprouts, carrots, greens—whatever is going.

St Clement's Chicken (serves 2)

This is a useful dish because it does not require any special wheat-free stock. The fruit juice makes sure the chicken is moist and it can be eaten hot or cold—ideal for a picnic, lunchbox or as a dish someone without wheat-free experience can cook easily. Serve one portion hot and leave the other to eat cold the following day. A good alternative to Christmas turkey.

2 fresh chicken quarters	1 large orange
ground cinnamon	Salt and freshly ground black pepper
3 teaspoons olive or sunflower oil	Parsley or watercress for garnish
1 large lemon	

Method: Skin the chicken (discard skin) and rub in a little salt, pepper and cinnamon. Use kitchen paper to grease an ovenproof casserole with 1 teaspoon oil. Place the chicken in the casserole. Grate the rind from half the orange and sprinkle over the chicken. Peel and chop the flesh. Cut the lemon in half and squeeze one half over the chicken. Peel the other half and chop the flesh. Add both kinds of flesh to the casserole. Drizzle over the remaining oil from a teaspoon and put on the lid. Cook at Gas 5/190°C/375°F for about an hour, until tender. Garnish and serve hot with plain boiled rice or potatoes, peas and carrots, or cold with a side salad of lettuce, watercress, and oil/lemon juice vinaigrette and cold rice or new potatoes.

Kebabs (serves 1)

A good meal to make if everyone else is having something wheaty and different. You will need the use of the grill and cooked, plain boiled rice. Don't put the kebabs too near the source of heat as this only cooks the outside.

1 skinned chicken breast or 4 oz (100 g) grilling steak

1 fresh tomato, quartered

¼ green pepper, deseeded and cut into pieces

½ medium onion, cut into segments

1 medium-sized mushroom, quartered

Grated rind and juice of ½ lemon

2 teaspoons soft brown sugar

2 teaspoons wheat-free soy sauce

Freshly ground black pepper

Method: Cut the meat into small, bite-sized pieces. Thread on to 2 skewers with the vegetables. Mix the lemon juice, rind, oil, sugar, wheat-free soy sauce and seasoning. Brush half over the kebabs and cook under a moderate grill for about 15 minutes. Brush the kebabs with the other half of the sauce mixture and grill on the other side for about ten minutes. Serve on a bed of hot boiled rice with a green side salad.

CHAPTER 6

Main Meals Without Meat

Use the vegetable and salad suggestions from the previous chapter with recipes in this one. Leeks and spinach go well with fish, also peas, carrots and broccoli. Greens, sprouts and cauliflower are better accompanying nut rissoles or used in stir/fry.

Fish Baked with Lemon (serves 1)
A good recipe for a cook who is not used to wheat-free cooking.

Sunflower oil for greasing	Rind of ½ an orange, finely
1 portion cod fillet (plain)—	grated
about 4–5 oz (100–125 g)	Freshly ground black pepper
Juice of ½ lemon	1 teaspoon freshly chopped
1 small knob of butter	parsley

Method: Grease a small ovenproof dish. Put in the fish. Squeeze over the lemon juice. Sprinkle over the rind and pepper. Top with the butter and bake uncovered in a preheated oven Gas 5/190°C/375°F, middle shelf for about 15 minutes. Serve with grilled tomatoes, peas and boiled potatoes. Just before you bring it to the table, sprinkle the parsley over the fish and potatoes.

Savoury Custards (serves 1)
These are tasty quiches without the pastry. They lend themselves to great variety and can be baked in little ovenproof dishes that can be covered and packed in a lunchbox. Good cold with salad or hot with hot vegetables. They can be made the day before and stored overnight in the refrigerator.

Method: Put an egg in a small basin with ½ pint (150 ml) milk and whisk to combine. Pour into a small ovenproof dish greased with sunflower oil. Put in the filling. Bake in a preheated oven Gas 5/190°C/375°C for about 30 minutes, until set, on the middle shelf.

Fillings

Tomato: 1 tomato sliced.

Spinach: 2 heaped tablespoons cold, cooked spinach, squeezed dry. Put in the bottom of the dish and pour the egg mixture over it.

Mushroom: 2 sliced mushrooms.

Herb: 1 level teaspoon finely chopped fresh herbs.

Cheese: 1 slightly heaped tablespoon grated cheese.

Watercress: handful of fresh watercress sprigs, chopped coarsely.

Prawn: 1 heaped tablespoon defrosted prawns and 1 teaspoon finely chopped parsley.

Tuna and Tomato: 1 heaped tablespoon tuna (canned in oil, not sauce, and drained) flaked, and 1 tomato, sliced.

Salmon with Watercress Sauce (serves 2)

3 tablespoons dry white wine

2 fresh salmon steaks

Sauce:

1 bunch watercress, chopped coarsely

Just over 2½ fluid oz (75 ml)/¼ pint milk

2 level teaspoons cornflour (pure maize) blended with 1 tablespoon cold water

Watercress for garnish

Method: Pour the wine into a shallow pan and top up with water to half full. Place the salmon steaks in the liquid and bring to the boil. Simmer gently for about six minutes, turn the fish over carefully and cook on the other side for another six minutes. While the fish is cooking make the sauce. Put the watercress into a blender with the milk. Blend and pour into a small saucepan. Stir in the cornflour mixed with water and bring gently to the boil. Immediately reduce the heat while you stir and the sauce thickens.

Put the salmon onto warmed plates and spoon the sauce over part of them and on to the plate. Garnish with watercress and serve with broccoli and potatoes.

Cold Salmon

Cook the fish as for hot salmon but cook for only four minutes each side and leave to cool in the poaching liquid. This helps to keep the fish moist. Serve with homemade wheat-free mayonnaise (see Chapter 7), salad and boiled potatoes.

Savoury Rice with Prawns and Vegetables (serves 2)

7 oz (200 g) rice, cooked and kept hot

2 teaspoons olive oil

2 spring onions, chopped

½ clove garlic, crushed

3 canned, peeled plum tomatoes, chopped

½ small courgette, chopped

Juice of ½ lemon

1 oz (25 g) button
  mushrooms, chopped
1 tablespoon chopped
  parsley

Freshly ground black pepper
3 oz (75 g) peeled prawns
Lemon wedges to garnish

Method: Fry the onions in the oil while you stir for two or three minutes. Stir in the garlic, tomatoes, courgette, mushrooms and lemon. Cook while stirring for about five minutes. Add the parsley, seasoning and prawns. Heat through gently for three minutes. Stir into the hot rice and serve garnished with wedges of lemon and parsley sprigs.

Fish and Healthy Chips (serves 1)

1 portion cod or haddock
Pure maize flour (wheat-free
  cornflour)

Sunflower oil
2 medium-sized potatoes

Method: Make Healthy Chips (see p. 50). Ten minutes before the chips are ready, dust the fish in cornflour and fry in a little hot sunflower oil on each side, turning once, about five minutes each side. Serve with the chips on hot plates. Have ready boiled broccoli and peas and, for colour, wedges of grilled tomato.

Sweet and Sour Fish (serves 2)

Small knob fresh ginger
  (about the size of a sugar
  cube) peeled and chopped
  finely
2 teaspoons sunflower oil.

1 teaspoon pure maize flour
  (wheat-free cornflour)
2 portions haddock cut into
  small chunks

Sauce:

½ medium can peeled plum
  tomatoes, drained and
  chopped
1 tablespoon wheat-free soy
  sauce
2 teaspoons tomato purée

1 teaspoon pure maize flour
  (wheat-free cornflour)
2 tablespoons water
3 teaspoons sherry
1 teaspoon brown sugar

Method: Rub the fish with the maize flour and ginger mixed, and fry in the hot oil, turning once, for about three minutes each side. Take out of the pan and keep warm. Put the tomatoes and wheat-free soy sauce into the pan. Combine the purée, maize flour, water, sherry and sugar in a small basin and pour over the tomato mixture. Stir while you cook, until thickened. Serve poured over the fish, on a bed of cooked rice mixed with 1 egg, scrambled. Also serve stir/fry vegetables.

Stir/Fry Vegetables

1 spring onion, chopped
¼ portion broccoli
   florets
½ small carrot sliced thinly

¼ green pepper cut into
   strips
About 5 mangetout peas
¼ teaspoon sesame oil
1 teaspoon sunflower oil

Method: Mix the two oils and heat in a wok or similar pan. Put in the onion and stir while you fry and turn the vegetables over for two minutes. Add the rest of the vegetables and 2 tablespoons water. Continue cooking in this way for another five minutes and serve hot with the fish dish above.

Nut Rissoles (makes 2)

These are the butt of vegetarian jokes! However, they are nutritious, inexpensive and tasty. Serve with red gravy (see Chapter 7) and spring greens, carrots and potatoes for a robust dinner.

½ medium onion, finely
   chopped
1 oz (25 g) almonds, finely
   ground
1 heaped tablespoon cooked
   rice or wheat-free
   breadcrumbs

2 teaspoons olive oil
¼ teaspoon fresh thyme
   or sage, finely chopped,
   or 3 pinches dried
1 teaspoon wheat-free soy
   sauce

Salt and freshly ground	1 medium-sized fresh
black pepper to taste	tomato, chopped
½ beaten egg	1 tablespoon sunflower oil

Method: Fry the onion gently in the olive oil for three or four minutes. Put into a basin with other ingredients except the sunflower oil and mix well with a fork. Form into rissoles using a spoon or a mould. Heat a tablespoon sunflower oil in a frying pan. Fry gently on each side for three minutes and serve hot as suggested. Can also be eaten cold with salad. If you find them difficult to shape, try sausage shapes instead.

Take care with the soy sauce—it must be a wheat-free brand.

Cauliflower and Broccoli Cheese (serves 2)

½ medium cauliflower	4 oz (100 g) tasty cheddar
1 head of broccoli	cheese, finely grated
1 oz (25 g) butter	1 teaspoon (genuine) French
1 fl oz (20 ml) milk	mustard
1 oz (25 g) pure maize flour	
(wheat-free cornflour)	

Genuine French mustard will be wheat-free. Mustard made in the UK usually has wheat added, even if it is labelled 'French'.

Method: Cut the cauliflower and broccoli into florets. Cook the cauliflower florets in boiling water for four minutes and then put in the broccoli and cook for another five or six minutes until both are cooked but still slightly crisp. Drain and put into a warmed ovenproof dish and keep warm. Put the butter into a saucepan and melt. Liquidise the milk, cornflour and mustard and pour into the pan. Heat and stir until it has thickened. Take off the heat and sprinkle in half the cheese. Stir without heating until melted and absorbed. Pour over the cauliflower and broccoli. Sprinkle the remaining cheese over the top and bake in a hot oven for ten minutes or put under the grill to melt and crisp the cheese. Serve with jacket potatoes and grilled tomatoes.

Cheese and Potato Pie (serves 1)
A simple vegetarian dish to serve with vegetables or a salad. If you are serving to a vegetarian, then be sure to use vegetarian cheese. Try your health food shop if the supermarket doesn't sell it.

2 medium potatoes, boiled and mashed (hot)
2 heaped teaspoons wheat-free margarine
Salt and freshly ground black pepper
4 chives, finely chopped
1 oz (25 g) finely grated cheddar cheese
2 medium tomatoes, sliced
Parsley for garnish

Method: Season the mashed potato to taste with salt, black pepper and a pinch of nutmeg. Beat in the margarine and chives. Put into a small ovenproof dish and flatten with a knife. Sprinkle the cheese evenly over the top and cover with tomato slices. Bake in a preheated oven Gas 4/180°C/350°F for just 15 minutes. Garnish with parsley and serve immediately with peas and carrots or spinach. In summer, serve with a green salad.

CHAPTER 7

Gravies, Dressings and Sauces

Some kinds of food are inclined to be dry. To make them easier to eat, sauces and gravies are used for fish, meat and poultry. Sweet sauces are used with puddings and desserts to add colour and flavour as well as make them moist.

Sauces, gravies and some dressings are usually thickened with wheat flour, so, in these recipes, where appropriate, maize flour (cornflour) is used instead. Cornflour is not always just finely ground corn-on-the-cob or maize; sometimes other starches are mixed with it. You will need a brand that claims to be 'pure maize' or 'maize starch' only. For gravies, potato and rice flour can also be used but the latter needs finding in the health food shop rather than the supermarket.

GRAVIES

Look at 20 gravy mixes/cubes/powders in the supermarket and don't be surprised to see all of them contain 'starch' of some mysterious kind. Gravy by nature is a thickened liquid, so what more likely starch is there for this than wheat? Forget gravy mixes and powders and make your own gravy instead. It is really very easy and only takes a minute or two.

You will need both a wheat-free thickener and stock. Meat juices from the grill pan and roasting tin are used as a base. Tomato purée and herbs can also be useful, especially if there are no meat juices available.

There are three suitable wheat-free flours for thickening gravy, all of them fine. Potato flour (or farina as it is sometimes called) is just potato starch. If you have cold boiled potato available it can be mashed and used instead of the dry potato starch. Cornflour (wheat-free brand) is starch from corn-on-the-cob and rice flour is made from ground rice.

If you want to avoid lumpy gravy, mix your chosen thickener with a little water to make a paste. You will be able to get the lumps out easily at this stage. If the worst happens and you end up with lumpy gravy, put it into the liquidiser and blend it.

Plain Gravy (serves 1)
Use the meat juices from the grill pan or roasting tin. Strain off the fat. If there is a lot, use a gravy separator. Make a thin paste in a cup with 1 heaped teaspoon of maize flour (wheat-free cornflour), potato flour or rice flour and 2 tablespoons cold water. Add to the pan with a cup of fresh vegetable strainings. Use the back of the spoon to rub the surface of the pan or tin while you heat. This will release the meat juices. Stir for a moment while it thickens, adding 1 teaspoon wheat-free soy sauce. Serve quickly while it is hot.

71

Take care with the soy sauce and cornflour—they must be wheat-free.

Red Gravy (serves 1)
Sometimes there aren't any meat juices for a gravy base. Here's a cheerful gravy for such an occasion. Use with vegetarian roasts, rissoles or burgers, or with meat rissoles and burgers.

1 teaspoon tomato purée
1 heaped teaspoon wheat-free thickener—maize flour (wheat-free cornflour), rice or potato flour

2 tablespoons cold water
Fresh vegetable strainings
1 teaspoon wheat-free soy sauce or other stock of your choice

Method: Put the purée and thickener into a measuring jug with the water. Mix well and gradually stir in vegetable strainings until it reaches the ¼ pint (150 ml) mark. Pour into a small pan and bring to the boil while you stir. Turn down the heat and cook, still stirring for another minute until nicely thickened.

Take care with the soy sauce and the thickening—they must be wheat-free.

SALAD DRESSINGS

Vinaigrette Type
The easiest way to make these is in a clean screw-top jar. The method is the same for all kinds. Put ingredients into the jar, put the lid on firmly and shake well. Label and store in the fridge. Shake well before using.

Plain Dressing

2 tablespoons oil— sunflower or olive oil
2 grinds black pepper

Scant tablespoon wine or cider vinegar
½ teaspoon castor sugar

Use on green or mixed salads.

Oil and Lemon Dressing

1 tablespoon olive oil	Juice of ½ fresh lemon
1 tablespoon sunflower oil	2 grinds black pepper
1 level teaspoon sugar	

Use for salad eaten with fish or salads that contain rice.

Mayonnaise (makes ½ pint (300 ml))

Commercial types of mayonnaise often contain wheat as a thickener. Unless you know of a wheat-free brand, why not treat yourself to the homemade variety? It only takes a few minutes if you have a liquidiser and the resulting jar of creamy mayonnaise can be stored in the fridge for up to two weeks. Use for salads and to make Tartare Sauce. All ingredients should be at room temperature.

¼ pint (150 ml) sunflower oil	½ level teaspoon made genuine French mustard (wheat-free)
¼ pint (150 ml) extra virgin olive oil	3 pinches salt
1 egg	Freshly ground black pepper
1 egg yolk	1 tablespoon boiling water
2 tablespoons wine vinegar	

Method: Have ready the boiling water, a scrupulously clean screwtop jar and a measuring jug. Pour ¼ pint sunflower oil into the measuring jug. Add olive oil up to the ½ pint mark. Put the egg, egg yolk, half the vinegar, mustard and salt into the liquidiser. Blend for just a few seconds. Take out the centre cap and begin to put in the oils slowly in a thin stream as you switch on. When all the oil has been poured in the mayonnaise will be thick. Add the remaining vinegar to thin it and lastly the boiling water. It is important not to allow more than a few seconds more running of the liquidiser after the hot water is added. Pour/spoon into the screwtop jar, label and date it and put in the fridge. Use as required and if any is left over after two weeks, throw it away.

(See p. 14 for information on labelling food. Mayonnaise may be a health risk for some people as it contains raw egg. Pregnant women would do well to avoid it.)

Tartare Sauce
This is a sauce with a base of mayonnaise to serve with fried fish, scampi, or prawns.

½ small clove garlic
3 tablespoons mayonnaise
(as above recipe)
½ teaspoon lemon juice

2 slices cucumber, finely chopped
1 teaspoon finely chopped parsley

Method: Rub the cut end of the garlic around a small bowl and discard. Put all other ingredients into the bowl and mix well with a teaspoon. Make as required and throw away any left over.

SAUCES

Mint Sauce (serves 2–3)
Pick the leaves off a small bunch of fresh mint. Wash well and shake dry. Put on to a chopping board and chop finely with a sharp knife. Spoon into a small bowl or jug and add a scant tablespoon (or less) of wine or cider vinegar, 2 heaped teaspoons of sugar and a teaspoon of boiling water. Mix well with a teaspoon and serve with roast or grilled lamb.

Italian Tomato Sauce (2–3 portions)

¼ medium onion, finely chopped
3 teaspoons olive oil
1 clove garlic, crushed
1 medium-sized tin peeled plum tomatoes in tomato juice, chopped
1 teaspoon tomato purée

½ teaspoon dried oregano
½ teaspoon dried basil or 3 leaves fresh basil, finely chopped
1 small bay leaf
1 level teaspoon castor sugar
Salt and freshly ground black pepper

Method: Fry the onion in the oil for two or three minutes without letting it brown. Add the garlic and cook for one minute while you stir. Spoon in the tomatoes and juice. Stir well and put in the purée, oregano, basil, the bay leaf and sugar with seasoning to taste. Bring to the boil then turn down the heat and simmer gently for 15 minutes. Remove and discard the bay leaf.

Use for special wheat-free pizza, as a sauce for baked or fried fish, with grilled meat or on wheat-free pasta. A textured, rich, red sauce.

Take care with the tomatoes. They must be just plain and wheat-free.

Bolognese Sauce (2 servings)

If a wheat-free pasta is not available, serve this robust and popular sauce on rice or potatoes. Can be frozen after it has grown cold, for future use.

½ medium onion, chopped
Scant tablespoon olive oil
4 oz (100 g) lean, raw minced beef
½ stick celery, chopped
1 small carrot, coarsely grated
1 slice trimmed back bacon, cut into small pieces
1 teaspoon tomato purée

1½ tablespoons white wine
2 teaspoons wheat-free soy sauce or stock of your choice
1 tea cup water
Freshly ground black pepper to taste
1 good pinch nutmeg
3 peeled tomatoes, chopped

Method: Fry the onion in the oil, while you stir. Add the beef and bacon and stir/fry for two minutes or until the meat is no longer pink. Add all other ingredients and bring to the boil. Turn down the heat and simmer for 15 minutes to make a rich, thickened sauce. Serve hot as suggested with a sprinkle of Parmesan cheese.

Brown Sweet and Sour Sauce (2 servings)

Small piece fresh ginger, about the size of a sugar cube, chopped very finely
¼ pint (150 ml) pure pineapple juice
2 teaspoons wheat-free soy sauce
1¼ tablespoons wine vinegar
2–3 heaped teaspoons castor sugar (to taste)
2 teaspoons maize flour (wheat-free cornflour)
1 tablespoon water

Method: Put all ingredients into a small pan and stir well. Heat, stirring all the time; cook until thickened and a rich brown colour—about three or four minutes.

Take care if using cornflour—it must be wheat-free.

THICKENED SAUCES

White Sauce (makes ½ pint (300 ml))

4 heaped tablespoons low fat dried milk granules
½ pint (300 ml) water
1 level tablespoon maize flour (wheat-free cornflour)

Method: Sprinkle the milk into the water and stir to reconstitute, stirring out any lumps. Put three tablespoons of this milk into a cup with the maize flour and, using a teaspoon, mix to a smooth cream. Heat the milk gently in a heavy-based pan. Catch it before it begins to foam and rise up and take it off the heat. Stir in the cornflour mixture and return to a lower heat. Cook while you stir for two minutes but don't let it boil. Use the thickened sauce as a base for parsley, tomato, watercress and cheese sauce.

Take care with your brand of cornflour as it may contain starches other than maize.

Parsley Sauce
Make as for white sauce but add 1 heaped tablespoon freshly chopped parsley. Serve with grilled, baked, poached fish or boiled bacon.

Watercress Sauce

Make as for white sauce but add 2 heaped tablespoons freshly chopped watercress. Serve with fish such as baked or poached haddock, plaice, cod and salmon.

Tomato Sauce

Make as for white sauce but add four liquidised tomatoes, a pinch or two of sugar (to taste) and grind of black pepper. Serve with poached, baked or grilled white fish.

Cheese Sauce

Make as for white sauce but add 1 extra level tablespoon dried milk granules to the water. To the cooked sauce add a slightly rounded tablespoon of grated cheddar cheese and ½ teaspoon genuine French mustard. Stir without heating until it melts.

Take care with the mustard—it must be wheat-free.

SWEET SAUCES

Custard (makes ½ pint (300 ml))

Not all brands of custard powder are wheat-free, so unless you can find one, it is best to make your own.

2 heaped tablespoons low fat dried milk granules	1 level tablespoon maize flour (wheat-free cornflour)
½ pint (300 ml) water	
2 heaped teaspoons sugar (castor or granulated)	2–3 drops vanilla flavouring

Method: Sprinkle the milk into the water and stir to reconstitute. Make sure there are no lumps. Put 3 tablespoons of the milk into a cup with the maize flour and mix to a smooth cream. Heat the milk and sugar gently in a heavy-based saucepan, while you stir. Take it off the heat just before it boils and stir in the maize flour and flavouring. Return to a low heat and stir/cook for two minutes until the custard has thickened.

Take care if using cornflour—it must be wheat-free.

Chocolate Sauce

Make as for custard but omit vanilla flavouring. To the maize flour and water add 2 heaped teaspoons wheat-free cocoa. Mix and proceed as for custard.

Orange or Lemon Sauce

Make as for custard but omit the vanilla flavouring and add the finely grated rind of ½ lemon or ½ orange.

Apple Sauce (makes 2 portions)

Peel and core a cooking apple. Cut into thin slices and put into a small pan with a little water and 2 teaspoons sugar. Cook over a gentle heat for about eight to ten minutes until the apple is soft. Stir well and serve hot with roast pork or cold with slices of cold roast pork.

Raspberry Sauce

Wash a punnet of fresh raspberries and put into a liquidiser. Add 1 tablespoon water and castor sugar to taste. Use on wheat-free ice cream.

Melba Sauce

Prepare 1 punnet redcurrants and 1 punnet raspberries. Stew in very little water—just enough to prevent them sticking to the pan—until soft. Put into the liquidiser after cooling for a few minutes. Blend to a purée then put through a fine mesh sieve with the back of a wooden spoon. Sweeten to taste with castor sugar and eat freshly made if you can. Freeze any leftover sauce for later use.

Good on wheat-free ice cream for a treat.

Chocolate Sauce for Profiteroles

This recipe gives a liquid chocolate suitable for pouring or spooning over profiteroles, ice cream and over pears. Can be used hot over the ice cream.

1 oz (25 g) plain wheat-free cooking chocolate	½ teaspoon pure instant coffee granules
Water	2 oz (50 g) castor sugar

Method: Dissolve the coffee granules in a little water and put on one side. Break the chocolate into pieces and put into a small saucepan with 2 tablespoons water. Heat gently to melt the chocolate. Add another 2 tablespoons water, the coffee liquid and the sugar. Continue to heat gently while you stir until dissolved. Simmer very gently for another eight to ten minutes and leave to cool. Use on the day of making.

CHAPTER 8

Puddings, Sweets and Desserts

It won't be long before you appreciate the value of fruit as a worry-free dessert. All fresh fruit is wheat-free and there is variety all the year round; also it is extremely healthy food.

You will find a few treats in this chapter. Use them as treats and not everyday fare. Fruit should be a staple in a healthy diet, so try to eat at least three pieces or the equivalent every day. Enjoy it baked, as a fruit salad, with yoghurt or just on its own. Avoid the habit of a scoop of ice cream or cream each time you eat fruit. Enjoy it for its own sake, it is excellent fare.

FRESH FRUIT

Fresh fruit on its own, or with a little sugar if it is too sour, is always an easy pudding. Strawberries, raspberries, ripe cherries, apples, bananas, peaches, plums or nectarines only need washing and putting on a plate. Ripe melon needs peeling and the seeds removing. Cut in half, scoop out the seeds, then quarter and slice away the flesh. You can use a melon baller but this is rather wasteful. (Use the leftovers to make fruit juice.)

Peel a good sized ripe orange and separate into segments. Arrange in a wheel shape on a plate. Alternatively, cut away the peel and pith with a sharp knife, then cut out the segments leaving behind the membrane. Arrange the slices on a plate and squeeze the leftovers over them. Add a sprinkle of finely chopped crystallised ginger for variation.

Juicy fruit will need a fruit knife and fork. Serve kiwi fruit halves with a teaspoon and other fruits that need to be peeled with a sharp knife.

Summerfruit Meringue (serves 2)

1 cooking apple, peeled and cored	Sugar to taste
	1 egg white
1 portion frozen summerfruits	2 oz (50 g) castor sugar

Method: Put the thinly sliced apples into a pan with about 1 tablespoon water and cook while you stir for about eight minutes. Add the thawed summerfruits and heat through gently. Sweeten to taste and turn into an ovenproof dish. Beat the egg white until stiff and forming peaks. Stir in the castor sugar with a metal spoon and spread evenly over the fruit. Bake in a preheated oven Gas 2/150°C/300°F to crisp the meringue—about 30 minutes. Serve hot.

Exotic Fruit Salad (serves 4)

Unless this is made for four people it is rather wasteful. Serve for a dinner party or to the whole family.

1 orange	1 passion fruit
2 kiwi fruit	½ mango
1 small punnet strawberries	small tin pineapple chunks or
1 banana	½ prepared fresh pineapple

Method: Put all the fruits except the banana in the fridge to cool. Prepare the chilled fruit, putting the passion fruit on one side, and slice the rest thinly into a glass bowl. Cut the passion fruit in half, squeeze over the sliced fruit and sprinkle with a little sugar if the fruit is not sweet enough. Serve soon after preparation, adding the freshly sliced banana.

STEWED FRUIT

Some fruits need to be stewed as they are not suitable for eating raw—for example, rhubarb, cooking apples, blackberries, cooking plums, damsons, green gooseberries, unripe pears, greengages and apricots, sour peaches and so on. Prepare the fruit and put into a pan with a little water to stop it sticking. Heat through slowly and add sugar to taste. Simmer until soft. Add fresh orange juice to rhubarb and save adding a good deal of sugar.

Raspberry Dessert (serves 2)

½ lb (250 g) fresh or frozen raspberries

1 generous tablespoon ground rice

Castor sugar

Water

Method: Save two firm raspberries for decoration. Put the rest into a small pan and heat gently while you stir. The juice will soon begin to run out and can be used to cook the fruit. Bring to the boil, still stirring, then simmer until soft—about four minutes or less. Allow to cool a little, then purée in a liquidiser. Put back into the pan. Measure the ground rice into a cup with 2 tablespoons water and mix well. Stir into the raspberry mixture and bring to the boil. Keep stirring over a lower heat until it has thickened. Stir in sugar to taste and spoon into glass dishes. When cold, decorate with the raspberries and serve.

Apple Snow (serves 2–3)

    1 Jb (500 g) cooking apples   2 egg whites
      (Bramley seedlings are   Finely grated rind of 1
      excellent)   lemon
    Sugar to taste   2 tablespoons water

Method: Peel and core the apples. Slice thinly and put into a small saucepan with the water and lemon rind. Cook while stirring until soft. Beat with a wooden spoon to make a smooth purée and sweeten to taste. Add 1 extra heaped teaspoon of sugar and stir in. Whisk the egg whites until they are stiff and will stand in peaks. Use a metal spoon to stir into the cooled apple purée. Spoon into glass dishes and serve chilled from the fridge.

DRIED FRUIT

There is no season for dried fruit so it can be eaten all year round. Wash fruit well and soak overnight in water. The fruit will swell and can be cooked the following day with a little brown sugar. Cooking times vary according to the fruit but 20 minutes is about average. Dried apricots, pears, peaches, prunes, apples, sultanas, figs and raisins can be used. Usually a mixture is more interesting than a single fruit, although apricots are good on their own. For a special dinner fruit dessert, try the following recipe.

Dried Fruit Compôte (2 servings)

    Soaking water   2 tablespoons red wine
    4 oz (100 g) dried fruit salad   ½ lemon
    1 oz (25 g) dried apricots   ¼ teaspoon cinnamon
    A few raisins and sultanas   Brown sugar to taste
    ¼ pint (150 ml) water

Method: Wash the fruit in a colander and put into a bowl. Put in enough water to cover plus another 2 teacupfuls. Leave to soak overnight. Pare the lemon rind off and cut into long thin strips. Put into a saucepan with the ¼ pint (150 ml) water, wine and spice. Add a level tablespoon of sugar (or less) and the drained fruit. Bring to the boil then turn down the heat and simmer with the lid on for about 20 minutes. Drain the fruit through a fine mesh sieve, over a basin to catch the juice. Pour it back into the pan and simmer for about ten minutes to reduce and thicken. This will make a rich red syrup to pour over the fruit. Put into individual glass dishes and serve hot or cold.

BAKED FRUIT

Slow baking of fruit you would normally stew sometimes improves it beyond measure. Rhubarb with orange juice is a classic example, as the fruit stays in shape instead of disintegrating. Fresh apricots with a sprinkle of finely grated lemon rind have a fuller flavour than plain stewed. Stubbornly hard fruit such as cooking plums, hard peaches and pears may take an hour or more on a low heat, Gas 4/180°C/350°F in a covered casserole. Softer fruit such as apples (sliced) or bananas, will be ready in 15–25 minutes. Higher heat can be used in a conventional oven but the casserole should be put on the bottom shelf or lower. Mixtures of fruit can be baked also, such as blackberry and apple.

Baked Bananas with Passion Fruit (serves 1)
Uninspiring to look at but full of flavour and easy to prepare. Put it in to bake as you serve the main course.

Peel one large or two small bananas and put into a small ovenproof dish, slicing the fruit in half lengthways. Cut a ripe passion fruit in half and squeeze the juice and pips over the bananas. Do the same with half an orange. Sprinkle with a teaspoon of brown sugar and bake, uncovered, for

15–20 minutes at Gas 4/180°C/350°F. Serve hot. (Use up the other half of the passion fruit in a fruit salad.)

Stuffed Baked Apples (serves 2)

2 cooking apples	Cinnamon
1 heaped tablespoon	Brown sugar
sultanas	1 cupful boiling water

Method: Core the apples and cut a line round the middle. Stuff with a mixture of sultanas, brown sugar and a pinch of cinnamon. Put into an ovenproof dish and pour in the water. Sprinkle a little sugar over the tops of the apples and bake in a preheated oven Gas 4/180°C/350°F for 25 to 30 minutes. Serve hot with single cream.

Rhubarb Crumble (serves 2)

2 portions rhubarb (about 4 stalks)	2 generous tablespoons (15 g) ground rice
Juice of ½ orange	1 tablespoon soft brown sugar
Brown sugar to taste	
1 tablespoon sunflower oil	2 teaspoons ground almonds

Method: Cut the rhubarb into short lengths and put into a saucepan with the orange juice. Sweeten to taste. Heat and stir to release the juice from the fruit. Cook for about ten minutes or until the fruit has softened. Put into an ovenproof dish and keep warm in the oven while you make the crumble. Put the oil, almonds and rice into a bowl and rub in until the mixture resembles breadcrumbs. Sprinkle in the sugar and spread lightly over the fruit. Make a hole in the centre to let out the steam. Bake in a preheated oven at Gas 7/220°C/425°F for about ten to twelve minutes. Serve hot or cold.

Yoghurt and Honey Fruit Ice Cream

This kind of ice cream is about as low in fat as possible and without egg yolks. Use as an occasional treat, not a staple food.

1 oz (25 g) frozen raspberries, strawberries or summer fruits, defrosted	3 tablespoons runny honey
	8 fl oz (250 ml) thick, creamy yoghurt, natural flavour
2 tablespoons orange juice	

Method: Put all ingredients into a liquidiser and blend quickly. Spoon the mixture into a suitable container, put in the freezer and chill for about one-and-a-half hours until firm but not rock hard. Cut into pieces with a knife and blend once more. Put back into the container, cover and chill again in the freezer. Defrost a little at room temperature for 15 minutes before serving.

Christmas Pudding

Christmas pudding can contain wheat breadcrumbs and wheat flour. This recipe will give you a pudding indistinguishable from the ordinary kind so you can make a large one for all the family.

¼ pint (150 ml) sherry	4 oz (100 g) chopped, stoned prunes
2 oz (50 g) barley flour	
2 oz (50 g) ground rice	2 eggs
2 oz (50 g) breadcrumbs made from homemade wheat-free bread	4 oz (100 g) currants
	4 oz (100 g) sultanas
1 teaspoon mixed spice (wheat-free)	2 oz (50 g) chopped dried apricots
1 level teaspoon pure cinnamon	4 oz (100 g) chopped shelled almonds
1 level teaspoon freshly grated nutmeg	Grated rind of 1 small lemon
4 oz (100 g) butter	Juice of 1 small lemon
4 oz (100 g) brown sugar	Grated rind of 1 orange
4 oz (100 g) grated apple	1 generous tablespoon black treacle
1 small carrot, finely grated	

Method: Melt the butter and put into a large bowl with all other ingredients. Stir well and leave covered overnight. The next day put into 1 large or 2 small pudding basins. Cover with foil and tie on with suitable string. Steam in a large saucepan with water halfway up the bowls and a grid underneath them. Keep topping up with boiling water while they steam for about six hours. Allow to cool on a wire rack, still in the basins. Take off the foil and renew. Store in a cool, dry place and steam for another one-and-a-half hours on Christmas Day. Tastes best one week after making. Serve with homemade wheat-free brandy butter and wheat-free custard (p. 77).

Brandy Butter
Avoid commercial brands. It is easy to make and can be made the day before and stored in the fridge. Serve to the whole family.

4 oz (100 g) unsalted butter	4 tablespoons brandy
6 oz (175 g) icing sugar	

Method: Cream the butter until white, then gradually beat in the sugar and brandy. Cover and store in the fridge.

Fruit Jellies (2 servings)
Make your own fruit juice by liquidising fresh fruit with water and add castor sugar to taste. Avoid kiwi fruit and pineapple which contain a natural anti-setting enzyme. Raspberries, peaches, red and black currants, strawberries, oranges or a mixture are all suitable. If planning fruit jelly as part of a packed meal, leave it to set in the container in which it will travel.

½ pint (150 ml) fruit juice	¼ oz (7 g) powdered gelatine

Method: Put about 2 tablespoons of the juice (cold) into a basin and sprinkle in the gelatine. Leave to soften for five minutes. Heat the remaining juice in a small pan but don't let it boil. Take off the heat and pour into the gelatine mixture while you stir. Continue until you are sure all the gelatine has dissolved. Pour into one or two glass dishes and leave to cool. Move to the fridge as soon as it is cold and allow to set. Use within a few hours of setting and serve chilled from the fridge.

Jelly Trifle
Use a crumbled sponge bun made with Trufree No. 7 S.R. wheat-free flour (see p. 94). Put into the bottom of a glass dish. Pour over jelly (as above) and leave to set. When cold top with homemade wheat-free custard (p. 77). Serve from the fridge.

CHAPTER 9

Cakes, Biscuits and Cookies

The kind of food featured in this chapter, if eaten every day, prevents it being special. Use most of the recipes only to make special food for celebrations. The fruit cakes make good packed lunch or picnic food. As a general policy, eating a lot of high-sugar, high-fat food won't make anyone healthy just because it is wheat-free. However, eating it occasionally for a treat is acceptable.

Carrot Cake (makes 6 slices)

¼ teaspoon nutmeg
½ teaspoon cinnamon
3½ oz (90 g) ground rice
1 oz (25 g) cornflour
½ oz (15 g) gram (chickpea) flour
3 pinches cream of tartar

2 good pinches bicarbonate of soda
2 oz (50 g) raisins, cut in half
1 oz (25 g) chopped walnuts
2 oz (50 g) polyunsaturated margarine, melted and cooled

3 oz (75 g) finely grated fresh carrot	1 generous tablespoon set honey
2 oz (50 g) soft brown sugar	1 egg beaten

Method: Mix the first seven (dry) ingredients in a bowl. In a second bowl mix the fruit, nuts, margarine, carrot, sugar and honey. Add the dry mixture and egg and mix well together to make a thick batter. Turn into a 6″ (15 cm) diameter cake tin, greased and floured with ground rice. Put into a preheated oven at Gas 4/180°C/350°F on a shelf above centre and bake for about 45 minutes or until a skewer comes out clean. Leave in the tin for five minutes then loosen the sides with a knife and turn out on to a wire rack to cool. Eat freshly baked. Any left over can be wrapped in individual slices and frozen for later use.

For a celebration the top of the cake can be iced.

Orange Icing

¾ oz (22 g) soft margarine	finely grated rind of ¼ of an orange
1½ oz (40 g) caster sugar	

Method: Beat the margarine to a cream. Add the sugar and beat again. Stir in the rind. Spread over the cake and leave to set before cutting.

Dundee Cake

Rye, barley and oat flours are rather too heavy for cakes and do not bind well. Buckwheat and cornflour don't bind at all so won't hold up the fruit. Here is a moist fruit cake very similar in appearance, taste and texture to the traditional wheat flour version. It freezes well so slices can be wrapped individually and stored in the freezer until required. A good traveller that makes a popular lunchbox snack.

Sunflower oil for greasing
2½ (65 g) wheat-free margarine
¼ pint (250 ml) orange juice

Flour Blend
1 oz (25 g) soya flour
4½ oz (115 g) ground rice
1 level tablespoon maize flour (wheat-free cornflour)

Fruit
8 oz (250 g) dried mixed fruit (washed in a colander and drained)

Decoration
1 oz (25 g) split almonds

3 oz (85 g) cored eating apple
1½ oz (40 g) fresh carrot
½ oz (15 g) instant yeast
1 tablespoon sugar

1 level teaspoon wheat-free mixed spice
2 oz (50 g) ground almonds

Grated rind of 1 lemon and 1 orange
2 oz (50 g) glacé cherries, well rinsed

Method: Grease a 6"–7" (15–16 cm) round cake tin. Put the margarine and fruit juice into a small pan and put over a low heat to melt the fat.

Take off the heat and leave until lukewarm, then pour into the liquidiser goblet. Cut the apple and carrot into slices and add to the liquid. Blend to a smooth, thick batter. Mix the yeast and sugar with the flour blend ingredients, in a large bowl. Pour in the mixture from the liquidiser and mix with a wooden spoon. Stir in the dried fruit and rinds. Spoon into the prepared cake tin, decorate with the split almonds and bake in a preheated oven Gas 4/180°C/350°F for about 1 hour. Test to see if it is done with a skewer. If it needs a little longer, cover with greaseproof paper and lower the heat. Bake a few minutes more. Leave to cool in the tin. When quite cold store in an airtight container and eat within 4 or 5 days.

Celebration Fruit Cake
A rich, dark cake, heavy with fruit. Cover with marzipan and ice for Christmas, birthdays, weddings, etc. Don't be afraid to pass this around as it is indistinguishable from cake made with wheat flour.

6 oz (170 g) ground rice
2 oz (50 g) soya flour
1 oz (25 g) cornflour
1 oz (25 g) gram (chickpea) flour
1½ teaspoons mixed spice
½ teaspoon cinnamon
4 oz (100 g) ground almonds
2 × 7 g sachets instant yeast
5 oz (150 g) polyunsaturated margarine
½ pint (300 ml) unsweetened orange juice
½ teaspoon almond flavouring
3 oz (75 g) soft brown sugar
2 medium eating apples, chopped including peel and core
3 oz (75 g) finely grated fresh carrot
14 oz (400 g) dried mixed fruit
2 oz (50 g) glacé cherries, rinsed and chopped
grated rind of 1 lemon
finely grated rind of 1 orange

Method: Put the eight ingredients for the flour blend into a large bowl and mix well. Warm the orange juice and margarine in a small pan over a gentle heat until the margarine has melted. Stir and put aside to cool down to lukewarm. When cool enough, pour into the liquidiser goblet. Also add the almond flavouring, sugar, apple and carrot. Blend and pour over the dry ingredients. Mix well then add the fruit and rinds. Stir in well. Have ready a 7″ (17.5 cm) diameter cake tin, greased and lined with greaseproof paper. Bake in a preheated oven Gas 4/180°C/350°F, on a shelf above centre for about one hour or longer. Test to see if it is done with a skewer. If it comes out clean the cake is ready. Leave to cook on a wire rack still in the tin. When cold, take out of the tin and wrap in a double layer of greaseproof paper. After two days open it up and prick the top of the cake with a fork. Dribble in 2 tablespoons of sherry and wrap it up again to store in an airtight container. Finish and eat within a week.

Rich Chocolate Cake
A celebration cake suitable for family and friends.

3 oz (75 g) ground rice
2 oz (50 g) cornflour
2 oz (50 g) barley flour
½ level teaspoon cream of tartar
1 level teaspoon bicarbonate of soda
2 tablespoons cocoa (wheat-free)
5 oz (150 g) caster sugar
2 tablespoons golden syrup
6 tablespoons sunflower oil
6 tablespoons milk
2 eggs, beaten
apricot jam

Method: Grease and flour (with barley flour) 2 × 7" (18 cm) sponge tins. Put the first seven (dry) ingredients into a bowl and mix well. In a basin mix the syrup, oil and milk. Whisk in the eggs. Pour into the dry ingredients and mix to a sloppy batter. Pour half into each tin and put in a pre-heated oven Gas 4/180°C/350°F, on a shelf above centre for 30–35 minutes. (They will spring back if pressed gently with a finger when done.) Take out of the oven but leave in the tins for five minutes then turn out on to a wire rack to cool. Sandwich together with jam.

Topping

1½ oz (40 g) polyunsaturated margarine or butter
3 oz (75 g) caster sugar
finely grated rind of ½ of an orange
1 oz chopped, toasted hazlenuts

Method: Beat the fat to a cream then stir in the sugar and beat again. Fold in the rind and spread over the top of the cake. Scatter the nuts over and press in lightly. Leave to set before cutting the cake. Store the finished cake in an air-tight container and use within a few days. To serve, put on a plate lined with a paper doily. Take care with the cocoa—not all brands are wheat-free.

Victoria Sponge (makes 8 slices)

4 oz (100 g) ground rice
2 oz (50 g) cornflour
2 oz (50 g) barley flour
½ level teaspoon cream of tartar
1 level teaspoon bicarbonate of soda
5 oz (150 g) caster sugar
2 tablespoons golden syrup
6 tablespoons sunflower oil
6 tablespoons milk
2 eggs, beaten
1 teaspoon vanilla flavouring
jam for filling
icing sugar for dusting

Method: Grease and flour (with barley flour) 2 × 7″ (18 cm) sponge tins. Mix the first six (dry) ingredients in a bowl. In a basin whisk the syrup, oil, milk, eggs and flavouring. Combine the two mixtures and beat to a sloppy batter. Pour half into each prepared tin and bake in a preheated oven Gas 4/180°C/350°F, above centre of oven. Bake for about 30 minutes. Test to see if they are done by pressing lightly with the fingertips. If they spring back, they are ready. Turn out, upside down, on to a wire rack to cool. When cold, sandwich together with jam and dust with icing sugar. Store in an airtight container and eat within a week.

Cream Gateau
A showy but easily made celebration cake.

Make the Victoria Sponge recipe. Spread whipped cream over one half and cover with fresh raspberries, halved strawberries or drained canned peach or apricot halves. Place the other sponge on top and spread with more whipped cream. Sprinkle with toasted almonds. Use on the day it is made.

Sponge Buns (makes 6)

2½ oz (70 g) ground rice
1 oz (25 g) cornflour
2 oz (50 g) caster sugar
1 egg, beaten
2 oz (50 g) soft margarine
½ teaspoon cream of tartar
¼ teaspoon bicarbonate of soda
6 drops vanilla flavouring

Method: Line six patty tins with cake papers. Put all ingredients into a bowl and mix to a creamy consistency using a wooden spoon. Divide between the paper cases and bake in a preheated oven Gas 5/190°C/375°F for about 15–18 minutes, until well risen and golden. When baked take out of the oven and put carefully on a wire rack to cool. Store in an airtight container and eat within three or four days.

Eat still warm from the oven for a treat.

Crunchy Apricot Tart

Makes a good pudding as well as a teatime treat or snack.

Filling

6 oz (150 g) dried chopped apricots, soaked overnight	Finely grated rind ½ lemon Brown sugar to taste

Pastry

2 oz (50 g) wheat-free margarine	4 oz (100 g) ground rice Sunflower oil for greasing
3 oz (75 g) finely grated eating apple (mush)	1½ oz (40 g) chopped almonds

Method: Make the filling first. Cook the apricots for 10–15 minutes in the soaking liquid and sweeten to taste. Strain off excess juices and mash the fruit with a fork. Stir in the lemon rind. Make the pastry by blending the margarine and ground rice with a fork. Add the apple mush and knead in the bowl to make one ball of dough. Grease an oven-proof pie plate and put the dough in the centre. Flatten with your palm and then gradually press out with your fingers until the pastry covers the plate. Raise an edge all round. Spread with apricot mixture inside the tart, sprinkle with the chopped almonds and press them in slightly. Bake at the top of a preheated oven Gas 7/220°C/425°F for 20–25 minutes until the pastry is golden. Cut into wedges and serve hot or cold. Eat within two days and store in the fridge, covered.

Mince Tart
Make as for Apricot Tart but use wheat-free mincemeat (see Chapter 11) instead of the apricots for the filling.

Rock Buns (makes 4)

1 oz (25 g) wheat-free margarine	2 pinches wheat-free mixed spice
2 oz (50 g) ground rice	1 pinch cinnamon
½ eating apple finely grated	Grated rind ¼ lemon
1 tablespoon granulated or demerara sugar	3 drops almond flavouring
	2 teaspoons ground almonds
1 heaped tablespoon dried mixed fruit	Sunflower oil for greasing
	More sugar for sprinkling

Method: Blend the margarine and rice in a bowl, using a fork. Add the remaining ingredients and mix with a wooden spoon. Grease a baking sheet. Drop four spoons of the mixture on to it. Spread out with a knife into cookie shapes. Sprinkle with sugar and bake in a preheated oven at Gas 8/230°C/450°F on a shelf above centre for about 20–25 minutes. Leave to cool on the baking sheet for three minutes then remove to a wire rack, using a spatula. The cookies will go crisp as they cool down. Eat within two days or, preferably, warm from the oven.

Sesame and Honey Crunch (makes 12)

1 oz (25 g) sesame seeds	2 oz (50 g) melted wheat-free margarine
3 oz (75 g) medium oatmeal	
3 tablespoons runny honey	1 oz (25 g) soft moist sugar
	Sunflower oil for greasing

Method: Toast the sesame seeds in a heavy-based pan over a gentle heat for 2–3 minutes until they are slightly coloured. Add the oatmeal, honey, wheat-free margarine and sugar. Mix well and press into a well greased sponge tin or ovenproof dish. Bake in a preheated oven, Gas 4/180°C/350°F for 20 to 25 minutes above centre shelf.

Allow to cool in the tin for five minutes, then cut into wedges or squares. Leave to grow cold in the tin. When quite cold store in an airtight tin. Eat within three weeks. Good for the lunchbox.

Date and Apple Cookies

1 oz (25 g) wheat-free margarine
2 oz (50 g) ground rice
1½ oz (40 g) finely grated eating apple mush

1 oz (25 g) sugar
4 stoned chopped dates
Sunflower oil for greasing
More sugar for sprinkling

Method: Put the margarine and ground rice into a bowl and combine with a fork. Add the apple, sugar and dates. Knead and mix with a wooden spoon to form one large ball of dough. Grease a baking sheet and drop spoons of the dough onto it, leaving space around each one. Spread them out with a knife to make biscuit shapes about ¼″ thick. Bake in a preheated oven, middle shelf, Gas 8/230°C/450°F for about 20–25 minutes. Allow to cool for two minutes then remove to a cooling rack, using a spatula. The cookies will grow crisp as they cool down. Sprinkle with a little sugar to finish. Eat freshly baked.

Macaroons (makes 12)

3 oz (75 g) ground almonds
3 drops almond flavouring
2 heaped teaspoons ground rice
4 oz (100 g) castor sugar

1 egg white
rice paper
12 split almonds for decoration

Method: Put the nuts, ground rice, flavouring and sugar into a bowl, and mix together. Lightly beat the egg white in a cup and pour onto the nut mixture. Mix well to a firm consistency. Line baking sheets with the rice paper. Divide the paste into 12 equal pieces and roll into balls. Place on the rice paper leaving space round each one as they will spread during baking. Flatten slightly with a fork and press a split almond into the centre of each one. Bake in a preheated oven Gas 4/180°C/350°F for 20 minutes. Cool on the baking sheet. When cold trim off excess rice paper with kitchen scissors. Store in an airtight tin.

Nutjacks (makes 8)

2 oz (50 g) butter or soft wheat-free margarine
2 oz (50 g) soft brown sugar
1½ oz (40 g) golden syrup

4 oz (100 g) rolled oats
1 oz (25 g) chopped cashews, almonds or hazelnuts
Sunflower oil for greasing

Method: Put the butter, sugar and syrup into a small pan. Melt over a gentle heat. Stir well and add the oats and nuts. Grease a small shallow sponge tin. Turn the mixture into this and flatten off with a palette knife. Bake in a preheated oven Gas 4/180°C/350°F until golden brown—about 20–25 minutes. Leave to cool in the tin for two or three minutes. Cut into fingers and cool on a wire rack.

Dessert Biscuits (makes 12 delicate biscuits)

Commercial ice cream wafers are made from wheat. These light, crisp biscuits make a welcome substitute. See back of book for details of the special flour required.

1½ oz (40 g) ground rice
½ oz (15 g) cornflour
1 tablespoon caster sugar

¼ teaspoon vanilla flavouring
½ oz (15 g) polyunsaturated margarine
½ egg, beaten

Method: Put the first four ingredients into a bowl and mix well. Stir in the egg and beat to a smooth cream. Put teaspoons of the mixture on to a greased baking sheet, leaving plenty of space around each one to allow them room to spread. Use the back of a teaspoon to spread them out into circles or fingers. Put in a preheated oven Gas

6/200°C/400°F, for about eight minutes until golden brown around the edges. Cool on a wire rack. Store in an airtight container. Put into a hot oven for a minute to re-crisp as required. Serve with wheat free ice cream, sorbet, fruit salad and fruit fools.

Honey and Fruit Slices (makes 5)

1 oz (25 g) sesame seeds
2 oz (50 g) rolled oats
1½ (40 g) runny honey
2 tablespoons sunflower oil

3 stoned prunes or 6 dried apricot halves, chopped
½ oz (15 g) brown sugar
more sunflower oil for greasing

Method: Grease a small shallow tin or ovenproof dish. Mix all ingredients together and put into the prepared tin. Press down and bake in a preheated oven Gas 4/180°C/350°F for about 30 minutes when it should be golden brown. Allow to cool in the tin. Cut into slices and finish cooling on a wire rack. When cold store in an airtight container.

CHAPTER 10

Breads, Rolls, Scones and Crispbreads

Commercial mills process a variety of foods into flours—wheat, rye, barley, oats, nuts, rice, split peas and so on. It is inevitable that contamination with wheat will take place as it is impossible to remove all wheat dust after milling. Most wheat-free dieters will probably tolerate this small amount which is hardly measurable. However, for those who cannot, the only solution is to grind your own flour at home or to find a 'dedicated' mill where wheat is never ground (difficult). Extra-sensitive wheat-free dieters should also avoid the kitchen when wheat is being used for cooking as it can easily be breathed in and cause a reaction.

Flour milling at home

You will need an electric mill (expensive) or a hand mill for this. Alternatively, try your luck with a coffee grinder. These are designed to grind hard beans and will give you a coarse version of flour. Buy the rye, barley grains and whole oats at the health food shop.

Link with the Past

By baking bread with no wheat grains you will be following in the footsteps of your ancestors. Rye and barley bread were for centuries the most common form of bread in this country. Loaves were heavy and dense in texture— extremely chewy and healthy, but apt to wear down the teeth. It is only in the last century that the soft, white, light-textured wheat bread we consider usual fare has entered the scene. Our ancestors probably would not recognise it as bread, it is so far removed from what they ate.

Trinity Bread

You will be hard put to distinguish this new kind of bread from the homemade wholewheat variety. It is delightfully crusty, brown and nutty flavoured as well as easy to make. It takes its name from the three flours in it—rye, barley and maize.

1 teaspoon sugar	7½ fl oz (212 ml) warm
½ oz (15 g) instant yeast	water
3 oz (75 g) rye flour	1 tablespoon sunflower oil
3 oz (75 g) barley flour	Oil for greasing
3 oz (75 g) maize flour	More barley flour for
(wheat-free cornflour)	kneading
Good pinch salt	

Method: Put the sugar, yeast, flours and salt into a bowl. Mix and make a well in the centre. Pour in the warm water and mix with a spoon to a sticky dough. Knead on a worktop, using more barley flour, for three or four minutes. Put the dough back into the bowl and leave to rise in a warm place for one hour, covered with a clean tea towel. Knead again for four to five minutes and shape into a ball. Put on a greased baking sheet and flatten. Cut the top with a knife, dividing the loaf into three. Leave to rise in a warm place. When doubled in size, bake in a preheated oven Gas 6/200°C/400°F for about 35–40 minutes. Take out of the oven and turn upside down on the baking sheet to cool. Cut when cold and store in a bread bin. (Much better than a leaden mixture of rye and barley that produces a heavy brick!)

Trinity Rolls
Make as for Trinity Bread but divide the dough into ten equally sized pieces. Roll between your palms then flatten and put on a greased baking sheet. Brush with milk and sprinkle with sesame or poppy seeds. Leave to double in size in a warm place. Bake at Gas 7/220°C/425°F for about 15 minutes. Cool on the baking sheet, turned upside down. Eat freshly baked.

If baking for the freezer, only bake for ten minutes. Allow to grow cold on a wire rack and store, wrapped, in the freezer. When required, allow to defrost for several hours, then crisp in the oven for five minutes at Gas 7/220°C/425°F.

Flatbreads (makes 3 pieces/1 portion)

2 oz (50 g) ground rice	½ oz (15 g) polyunsaturated
1 oz (25 g) barley flour	margarine
2 good pinches bicarbonate	1 oz (25 g) fresh mashed
of soda	potato
3 pinches cream of tartar	2 tablespoons milk
1 level teaspoon caster sugar	

Method: Mix the first five (dry) ingredients in a bowl. Rub in the margarine then the mashed potato. Stir in enough milk to bind into a stiff, smooth dough. Put on to a baking sheet and shape into an oblong about ½" (1 cm) thick. Cut into 3 pieces and move them apart. Bake in a preheated oven Gas 7/220°C/425°F on the top shelf until golden brown—about 15 minutes. Cool on a wire rack. Eat on the day of baking to replace bread.

Wheat-Free Mixed Grain Bread (makes 1 small loaf)
Here's a new kind of bread that keeps well and is easy to make. The end result is very similar to ordinary barley bread made partly with wheat. Even so it is a robust, dense kind of bread.

4 oz (100 g) barley flour	1 tablespoon sunflower oil
2 oz (50 g) potato flour	¼ oz (7 g) easy-blend yeast
2 oz (50 g) rye flour	1 egg white
1 oz (25 g) oat bran	6 fl oz (175 ml) warm water
¼ teaspoon salt	More oil for greasing tin
1 teaspoon sugar	

Method: Put the flours, bran, salt, sugar and yeast into a large bowl. Mix well to blend. Add the oil and rub in with the fingers. Put the egg white into a jug with the water and whisk with a fork to combine. Make a well in the flour mixture and pour in the egg white/water. Use a wooden spoon to mix to a sticky paste. Put into a warm place to rise, covered with a clean tea towel. When doubled in size, turn out on to a worktop floured with more barley flour and knead for about four or five minutes until smooth. Grease a 1 lb (500 g) bread tin and put the dough into it, pressing it into the corners. Leave to rise in a warm place until up to the top of the tin. Bake above centre of a preheated oven at Gas 6/200°C/400°F for about 30–35 minutes. Turn out of the tin and cool on a wire rack. Store in a bread bin.

Corn Bread

Don't confuse fine cornmeal with cornflour as it is much coarser. Cornbread is a staple in some parts of America. It has a lovely golden colour and looks rather like a sponge when baked. It must be eaten freshly baked, warm from the oven. Eat with soup, a main meal or just on its own as a fill-you-up food. Health stores stock fine maize meal or corn meal. Often it is called Masa Harina and is made from corn-on-the-cob.

4 oz (100 g) fine maize meal
2 teaspoons soya flour
½ teaspoon wheat-free baking powder
½ teaspoon sugar

5 fl oz (150 ml) water
1 small egg, beaten
2 teaspoons sunflower oil
More oil for greasing tin

Method: In a mixing bowl put the maize meal, soya flour, baking powder and sugar. Mix and make a well in the centre. Pour in the water, egg and oil, stirring all the time to make a creamy batter. Oil an 8″ (20 cm) sponge tin and pour in the batter. Bake above centre of a preheated oven Gas 6/200°C/400°F for about 35 minutes, until the edges and top begin to turn brown. Eat cut into wedges.

Wheat-Free Dropscones (makes 7 or 8)

1 oz (25 g) potato flour
1 oz (25 g) fine oatmeal
2 oz (50 g) barley flour
1 teaspoon cream of tartar
½ teaspoon bicarbonate of soda

¼ teaspoon salt
1 oz (25 g) castor sugar
½ beaten egg
4 fl oz (125 ml) milk
2 teaspoons oil
More oil for greasing

Method: Put all ingredients except the oil into a liquidiser and blend to a smooth batter. Grease a heavy-based frying pan or griddle with sunflower oil and heat. Drop table-spoonfuls of the batter on to the hot surface and cook until bubbles appear. Turn over with a spatula and cook on the other side until golden brown. Put on a dish covered with a clean tea towel, folded over to keep them warm, until they are all cooked. Serve with butter and jam or runny honey. Eat freshly made.

Rye and Potato Crisps

Choose a floury potato such as King Edward that will mash easily. Anyone who enjoys potato crisps will like these giant crisps. Use instead of crispbreads.

8 oz (250 g) mashed potatoes	3 oz (75 g) rye flour
¼ teaspoon salt	Sunflower oil for greasing

Method: Beat the potato with a wooden spoon until there are no lumps, or press through a fine sieve. Add the salt and rye flour, kneading it in to form a sticky dough. Break off pieces of the dough and roll out as thinly as possible. (You will need to use plenty of rye flour for this as the dough will be very sticky.) Cut into shapes, then prick them all over with a fork. Heat a heavy-based frying pan or griddle. Grease lightly with oil and kitchen paper and cook quickly on both sides. Best eaten fresh. Easiest way to move them from worktop to pan is by spatula or fish slice.

Oat Crispbreads (makes 6)

4 oz (100 g) medium oatmeal	3 tablespoons cold milk
Pinch salt	More oatmeal for rolling out

Method: Put the oatmeal into a bowl with the salt. Mix well and put in the milk. Stir to make a soft dough. Sprinkle the worktop liberally with oatmeal and divide the dough into three. Roll each piece out thinly and trim neatly into squares or oblongs. Take the crispbreads off the worktop carefully, using a spatula. Have ready a heated griddle, heavy-based frying pan or pancake pan. A moderate heat is all that is required; if the pan is too hot the crispbreads will burn. Cook two at a time for two minutes, then turn them over and cook for just a minute on the other side. Cool on a wire rack and serve freshly baked.

Excellent with soup or cheese or in a packed lunch.

Try to make them all the same size and shape and they will look really professional. If you find it easier, use a pastry cutter.

Barley Flatbreads
Use instead of wheat bread.

1 heaped tablespoon barley flour	2 teaspoons sunflower oil
	Extra oil for greasing
1 heaped tablespoon buckwheat flour	Cold water
Pinch salt	More barley flour for rolling out

Method: Mix the two flours and salt in a bowl. Rub in the 2 teaspoons of oil with the fingertips. Add 2 tablespoons water and start to make a stiff dough, adding more water if required. Knead with your hands for about three minutes, then shape into a ball. Cut with a knife into four equal-sized pieces. Sprinkle the worktop with barley flour and roll out each piece until it is as thin as a chapati. Use a spatula to lay them on a hot oiled griddle or a heavy-based frying pan. Cook two or three minutes on each side.

CHAPTER 11

Miscellaneous

Homemade Stock
If you cannot find a suitable wheat-free, MSG-free stock, then you will have to make your own and freeze it for future use. Here are two recipes, one with meat and one with just vegetables.

Meat Stock
For this type of stock you will need bones or a carcase, carrots, onions and parsley. Put these into a saucepan with plenty of water and bring to the boil (any scum that forms can be skimmed off and discarded). Simmer gently with the lid on for 1–1½ hours. Strain off the liquid and reduce by bringing to the boil and simmering for another half-hour. If it is disappointing, add a little Marmite (yeast extract) to taste. Cool and freeze in small containers. Use as required.

Vegetable Stock

Fry a chopped onion in 1 tablespoon sunflower oil. Add a few sprigs of parsley, chopped carrots, celery, greens, mushrooms and tomatoes—everything except potato. Put in enough water to cover and bring to the boil. Simmer with the lid on for one hour. Strain into a bowl through a fine mesh sieve, pressing the vegetables with the back of a wooden spoon. Cool and freeze, in small containers. Use as required. To strengthen, add a little Marmite (yeast extract) to taste.

Homemade Lemonade

Wash, then cut up two lemons into thin slices. Put into a jug and pour boiling water from the kettle over them. Leave to stand, covered, for 12 hours or so. Strain off the liquid. Add sugar to taste and dilute with water. Store in the fridge and use within two days. A refreshing drink for hot weather.

Pancakes

1½ oz (45 g) ground rice	1 egg
½ oz (15 g) cornflour	¼ pint (140 ml) milk
pinch salt	sunflower oil for greasing pan

Method: Put all ingredients except the oil into a liquidiser and blend to a thin batter. Grease a frying-pan with a little oil and heat. When really hot pour in one third of the batter, tilting the pan to cover the base. Cook for two minutes, loosen with a spatula and turn over to cook on the other side. Keep warm while you make the remaining batter into two more. Serve rolled up with a little sugar and fresh lemon juice, or spread with sweetened stewed fruit and roll up. Serve as soon as possible on a warmed plate.

Yorkshire Pudding (makes 4 small puddings)

¾ oz (22 g) barley flour	½ egg, beaten
¼ oz (7 g) cornflour	1 tabespoon milk
pinch salt	1–2 tablespoons water

Method: Preheat oven at Gas 7/220°C/425°F. Mix the flours and salt in a basin. Whisk the egg and milk. Add to the basin and mix well. Put in enough water to beat to a thin cream. Spoon into 4 hot, oiled, small patty tins and bake on the top shelf for about 10–12 minutes. Serve hot with roast beef.

Stuffings

Savoury mixtures of wheat breadcrumbs, onion, herbs and sometimes fruit are used in poultry and boned meat. Commercial stuffings will almost certainly contain wheat. Here are a few recipes to cope with this problem. For a base use homemade wheat-free breadcrumbs made in the coffee grinder, or try cooked rice instead. Don't be afraid to serve to the whole family as they will make stuffings every bit as good as the wheat type.

Sage and Onion Stuffing

Mix 3 oz (75 g) cooked rice or wheat-free breadcrumbs with 1 tablespoon sunflower oil and 1 medium onion, chopped finely. Add four fresh sage leaves, finely chopped (or 1 teaspoon dried sage) and salt and freshly ground black pepper to taste. Mix well and turn into an oven-proof dish greased with sunflower oil. Bake in the oven at the same time as a chicken or joint of pork. When crisp and brown move down to the floor of the oven to keep hot.

Lemon and Thyme Stuffing

Make as for sage and onion stuffing but omit the sage and substitute thyme and the grated rind of a lemon.

Savoury Spreads

The commercial kind of spreads and pastes usually contain rusk made with wheat. You can make your own easily at home, as required.

Salmon Paste

Mash salmon (canned in water and drained well) and a little homemade wheat-free mayonnaise (or wheat-free commercial mayonnaise). Season with freshly ground black pepper.

Sardine Paste

Use sardines canned in oil and not sauce. Drain well and mash with a little fresh lemon juice and chopped parsley. Season with freshly ground black pepper.

Sardine and Tomato

Make as for sardine paste (above), but add a little wheat-free tomato purée.

Curried Egg Spread

Mash hard-boiled egg to a paste with a little homemade wheat-free mayonnaise (or wheat-free commercial mayonnaise). Sprinkle in wheat-free curry powder (see recipe p. 111) and season to taste with salt.

Egg and Cress Spread

Mash hard-boiled egg and stir in very finely chopped cress or watercress. Season with salt to taste.

Prawn Spread

Mash defrosted prawns with a little homemade wheat-free mayonnaise (or wheat-free commercial mayonnaise). Season with freshly ground black pepper to taste.

Curry Powder

Food for a sensitive digestive system is best without quantities of strong spices such as turmeric. Commercial curry powder and pastes usually contain a mysterious thickener, which is quite likely to be wheat. Here's a recipe for curry powder without either. If you are dubious about the chilli, it can be omitted. The spices must be labelled 'pure' and be a reputable brand or you could have a contamination problem. If you cannot get ground cardamom, buy the pods and use the seeds of about 12, crushed in a pestle and mortar.

1 level tablespoon each of ground cumin and cardamom	4 pinches chilli powder (optional)
½ level teaspoon cinnamon	Good grind of black pepper
	¼ teaspoon ground cloves

Method: Break open the cardamom pods and put the tiny seeds into a pestle and mortar. Grind to a powder. Add the remaining ingredients and mix well. Store in a cool dark place in an airtight jar. Label and date it. Use sparingly as a flavour.

CHRISTMAS

Christmas is usually a difficult time for the wheat-free dieter. All around, people will be tucking in to wheat fare—Christmas cake, sausages, stuffing, gravy, pudding, mincemeat tarts, party food, sandwiches, chocolates. This is the time to use the wheat-free versions (from this book) for Christmas cake, sausages, gravy, puddings, mincemeat and chocolates, marzipan, icing and sweets. Make for everybody and have a worry-free festive season.

Royal Icing (to cover a 9″ (225 mm) cake)
This recipe gives enough icing for one thin coat on top of

the marzipan and a thicker layer for finishing. Buy glycerine at the chemists.

3 egg whites	1 teaspoon lemon juice
1½ lbs (675 g) sifted icing sugar	1½ teaspoons glycerine

Method: Put the egg whites into a bowl and beat with a fork until frothy. Change to a wooden spoon and beat in half the icing sugar. Add the lemon juice, glycerine and the rest of the icing sugar. Beat to make it smooth and stand in peaks. Cover the bowl with a clean tea towel for a few hours. During this time air bubbles will disperse. Stir with a wooden spoon and spread on with a palette knife dipped first in hot water.

Christmas, Wedding or Christening Cake
Make the rich fruit cake from p. 92. Trim level with a bread knife. Turn upside down on a cake board. Spread with apricot jam or marmalade and cover with marzipan. Leave 24 hours to harden and ice with Royal Icing.

Sweet Mincemeat
Wheat flour often gets into commercially made mincemeat on the suet which is rolled in flour to prevent it going back to one sticky lump. Not only is this recipe wheat-free, it is also suet free and much better than any commercial mincemeat

3 oz (75 g) each of sultanas, raisins and currants, all washed well	1 medium apple, grated
	½ tablespoon each allspice, cinnamon and freshly
2 oz (50 g) soft brown sugar	grated nutmeg
2 tablespoons sunflower oil	Rind of 1 lemon, finely
1 oz (25 g) each chopped walnuts and almonds	grated
	Fresh orange juice

Method: Mix all ingredients together in a bowl. Moisten with orange juice. Mix again and spoon into jars. Put on

112

the lids and store in the fridge to use as required. Label and date. Keep no longer than five weeks.

Makes a nice Christmas gift for *everyone*, especially wheat-free dieters.

Almond Paste

Commercially made almond paste does not resemble the best homemade type at all and often contains wheat. Real almond paste is not bright yellow but a dark ivory colour. It is made rather like pastry and keeps well in the fridge for a few weeks. Leftovers can be used to stuff dates and make chocolates. Otherwise use to cover celebration cakes such as Christmas cake before icing.

6 oz (150 g) ground almonds	1 egg
2 oz (50 g) icing sugar	4 drops almond flavouring
1 teaspoon castor sugar	Icing sugar for rolling out
Juice of ½ lemon	

Method: Put the almonds and sugars into a bowl and mix well. Whisk the egg in a cup. Combine the lemon juice and flavouring. Add both mixtures to the almonds/sugars and knead to a paste. Roll out using more icing sugar.

Stuffed Dates

Remove the stones from dessert-grade eating dates (*deglet nour*) and fill the cavities with wheat-free almond paste.

CONFECTIONERY AND SNACKS

Chocolates

Melt wheat-free cooking chocolate very gently in a small dish over a pan of hot water. Roll small pieces of wheat-free almond paste (see above) into balls, flatten and then coat with the chocolate. Easiest way is to pierce with a skewer and dip into the melted chocolate. Leave to set on a lightly buttered plate. Press a split almond into the top of each one before the chocolate sets. Wheat-free cooking chocolate can be bought in milk, plain or white flavours. Check label carefully.

After Dinner Chocolate Mints
Use leftover royal icing. Flavour with peppermint flavouring and shape into balls. Flatten and dip into melted wheat-free plain cooking chocolate, using a skewer. Leave to set on greaseproof paper. Eat within two or three days of making.

Toffee
This often contains wheat flour, so homemade toffee is a must. Use as a treat, not a staple food. The secret of good toffee is to heat gently until all the sugar has dissolved. After that, boil quickly.

4 oz (100 g) brown sugar	2 generous teaspoons golden
¼ teaspoon maize flour	syrup
(wheat-free cornflour)	Butter for tin
2 oz (50 g) butter	

Method: Use a small, heavy-based pan to gently melt the butter. Put in the sugar, maize flour and syrup. Bring to the boil, slowly. When the sugar has dissolved, stir well and bring to the boil. Continue boiling for about 15 minutes or until it will set. To find out if it will set, take the pan off the heat and drop a teaspoon of the mixture into a cup of cold water. If it is not ready, continue to boil. Butter a shallow tin and pour in the mixture when ready. Leave to set, marking squares with a knife when cooling down. Cut into squares before it cools completely. Allow to grow cold and wrap individually in squares of greaseproof paper. Store in an airtight tin.

Roasted Nuts
Most commercial snacks contain some kind of 'starch' that it quite likely to be wheat. Many contain MSG which could

be made from wheat starch. Nuts roasted in coatings should be avoided as these are dubious for the wheat-free dieter. Try these simply roasted nuts and you won't feel deprived.

Put about 20 shelled (but not blanched) almonds on a baking sheet and bake on the top shelf Gas 6/200°C/400°F for six minutes, when they will be crisp and brown. Allow to cool. Serve as a nibble or snack. Cashews are also good roasted but not for as long—try four minutes.

Apple Chutney

Commercial brands of chutney often contain wheat and other undesirables such as MSG. If you don't have a wheat-free brand available, make this chutney as required. Recipe is for a 1 lb (500 g) jar but it is probably a good idea to put it into two smaller jars.

4 oz (100 g) onion, chopped	5 oz (125 g) brown sugar
Water	¾ oz (7 g) ground ginger
Cooking apples, peeled and chopped	2 tablespoons sultanas
	3 pinches salt
½ pint (300 ml) cider vinegar	2 good pinches cayenne pepper

Method: Put the onions into a small pan and cover with water. Bring to the boil and simmer for a few minutes until softened. In a separate pan put the apples and vinegar. Strain the onions, discarding the water. Add to the apples with remaining ingredients. Cook over a gentle heat, stirring frequently until thick. Put into clean, warmed jars and cover. Use as required. Remember to label and date it.

CHAPTER 12

Picnics, Packed Lunches, Celebrations and Menus

It may seem a chore, but packing a lunchbox or picnic is your only real guarantee of a nutritious meal that is wheat-free.

Forget the salty convenience snacks, chocolate bars and wheatbread sandwiches. Instead concentrate on packed meals which are healthy, colourful, tasty and varied, which will travel well.

Containers

A collection of small containers is helpful. Before anything goes in the kitchen rubbish bin decide whether you could use it for packing food. Cottage cheese pots, jars with screwtop lids, margarine containers and small bottles can be thoroughly cleaned and re-used several times. Kitchen departments in stores or kitchen shops should have a good selection of lidded containers and the supermarket sells throwaway shrinkwrap film and food bags.

Greaseproof paper is also useful for packing foods that are still warm. Some kind of container for the whole meal, which can be cleaned easily, is essential. Again, try kitchen departments and even the chemists. For hot weather use a 'cool box' and freezer pack.

Preparation

If preparing a picnic or lunchbox meal early in the morning is difficult, do it the night before and keep it in the fridge. Although not an ideal situation, this is a better solution than not bothering at all.

'Finger food' is easy to eat and so is 'spoon' or 'fork' food, but don't forget to pack the spoon or fork. If you know a suitable drink will not be available, take fruit juice, mineral water or a flask of tea or coffee and either dried milk or a small bottle of milk. Flasks can be used for hot or cold drinks and soups for winter.

Balance

A high-protein food such as cheese, egg, meat, fish or nuts should always be the base of a packed meal. Raw vegetable nibbles to eat with it are celery sticks, radishes, small tomatoes, courgette and carrot sticks, sprigs of watercress, lettuce leaves, spring onions and cauliflower florets. Wash, dry well and pack loosely. A wheat-free dip or dressing can be packed in a small container.

Dried fruits (well washed), such as apricots, peaches, stoned prunes, raisins and sultanas are easy to eat with the fingers and fresh fruit that travels well is ideal—apples, oranges, satsumas, clementines, bananas, cherries, grapes or kiwi fruit. Anchor them down well, otherwise they will collect bruises on the journey. Yoghurt, homemade jelly set in a container or a fruit salad in a screwtop jar can be packed with a spoon.

For the carbohydrate part of the packed meal, take a container with cooked rice, potatoes or wheat-free crispbreads/bread rolls. Any of the food from Chapter 9 or 10 is in the high carbohydrate category and can be packed neatly in a small container or wrapped in greaseproof.

Suggestions
Here are a few ideas for balanced packed meals to be eaten with spring water, or tea/coffee from a flask.

1   Cottage cheese, celery and carrot sticks, radishes, wheat-free crispbreads, dried apricots, almond macaroon, sweet, crisp apple.
2   Hard-boiled egg, or savoury custard (see p. 64), watercress sprigs, crisp lettuce leaves, small bottle of lemon vinaigrette, cold potatoes, tomato, orange, slice of wheat-free Dundee cake.
3   Mixed salad of flaked tuna (canned in oil, not sauce), cold rice, chopped celery, chopped spring onion, whole tomato, homemade fruit yoghurt, plain nuts and raisins.
4   Homemade wheat-free muesli with a separate small container of milk, cheddar cheese, celery sticks, banana.
5   Cold lean beef, pork or ham (without breadcrumb coating), cut into small squares; cold potato slices, chopped onion, sliced radishes, cauliflower florets, wheat-free vinaigrette in a small bottle. Apple, kiwi fruit (to cut in half and eat with a teaspoon).

Advice
Don't forget, variety is all important. Avoid the same kind of lunchbox day in day out. Any of the savoury spreads

from Chapter 11 can be used with wheat-free crispbreads/ bread rolls. Chapters 8 and 9 also have useful food to pack. Fresh fruit varies with the season and adds colour as well as vitamins.

Spoon, fork, mug, salt and tiny pepper mill, fruit knife, plastic plate or bowl, flask are all you could possibly need, apart from the actual food. After they are washed up, store them in the hamper or lunchbox and this will save running around trying to locate them when you are in a hurry. Keep the paper napkins handy. One of these is essential with a packed meal, especially if finger food is included.

CELEBRATIONS

Wheat-free dieters sometimes need to celebrate, just like anyone else. The difference is in the food they can use. Providing two celebration cakes, one with wheat, one without, can be rather awkward. It is better to put on a wheat-free one that everyone can enjoy (see p. 92 for Celebration Fruit Cake recipe).

Wheat-free food such as fruit can be used to make fruit salad which everyone finds acceptable. Dips with wheat-free mayonnaise or vinaigrette are always popular. Any of the food from this book is suitable for people who *can* eat wheat.

If giving a party, serve mostly wheat-free food and a few foods made with wheat. However, take care to mark the foods in some way so the wheat-free dieter doesn't make a mistake.

For children's parties, serve homemade jelly and ice cream, wheat-free sponge buns (iced) and crisps, as a wheat-free basis which will suffice for the wheat-free dieter. Top up with other foods from this book so that the whole amount of party food is wheat-free.

It is very easy to arrange wheat-free dinner parties so

that everyone has the same. Use the recipes from Chapters 4, 5, 6, 7 and 8 for a worry-free evening. Finish with *After Dinner Chocolate Mints* from Chapter 11. Serve with rolls from Chapter 10.

Here are some wheat-free dinner party menus using recipes from this book:

Tomato and Basil Soup

Roast Lamb
Mint Sauce
Boiled New Potatoes
Broccoli
Peas

Baked Apricots or
Rhubarb Crumble

    *   *   *

Water-lily Melon

Cold Salmon and
   Mayonnaise
Boiled New Potatoes
Green Salad
Tomatoes

Fresh Strawberries

Avocado and Orange

Baked Fish with Lemon
Boiled New Potatoes
Broccoli
Grilled Tomatoes

Summerfruit Meringue

    *   *   *

Mushroom Soup

Roast Beef
Wheat-free Yorkshire
   Pudding and gravy
Sprouts
Peas
Roast Potatoes

Stuffed Baked Apples

MENUS

The key to healthy eating is to enjoy meals that are low in fat, sugar and salt and high in fibre, with plenty of fresh fruit and vegetables. To help you, here are suggestions for main meal menus which are well balanced and healthy. **Recipes are all in the book unless indicated.**

120

Tomato Soup

Shepherd's Pie or
   Beefburgers
Gravy
Peas
Carrots
Cabbage

Rhubarb Crumble

*   *   *

Vegetable Soup

Ham or Prawn Omelet
Spinach
Healthy Chips or Boiled
   New Potatoes

Dried Fruit Compote

*   *   *

Parma Ham with Fruit

St Clement's Chicken
   (cold)
Salads inc. Lettuce
Baked Jacket Potato
Mayonnaise

Stewed Summerfruits

Grapefruit

Roast Lamb and Mint
   Sauce, Gravy
Roast Potatoes
Spring Greens or Sprouts
Carrots

Crunchy Apricot Tart

*   *   *

Chicken Soup

Fish and Healthy Chips
Peas and Carrots
Grilled Tomatoes
Spinach

Raspberry Dessert

*   *   *

Pea Soup

Kebabs
Boiled Rice
Green Salad with
   Dressing

Fresh Fruit Salad

When making your own combinations for three-course meals, try to include one fruit course, plenty of vegetables including one leafy green one, rice or potatoes and a low fat, low sugar pudding.

Useful Information

GLUTEN

One of the substances found in wheat is a protein called *gluten*. By washing wheat flour it is possible to remove most (but not all) of the gluten, leaving a pure white powder— *wheat starch*.

If you are trying to follow a wheat-free diet, don't make the mistake of believing products labelled 'gluten-free' are also wheat-free. They are quite likely to be made from wheat-free starch and are therefore unsuitable for the wheat-free dieter. Do scrutinise ingredients labels carefully before buying and eating such commercial diet foods—the products may not be what they seem.

MILK-FREE DIET

Some wheat-free dieters have the added problem of following a milk-free diet (or dairy-free diet as it is sometimes called). If this is the case, find a milk-free brand of margarine to use in the recipes instead of ordinary margarine and butter. Do not use cream or cheese; substitute soya milk for the ordinary cow's milk in the recipes. Sometimes water or fruit juice can be used instead of milk—for example, on breakfast cereal. Your local health food shop is sure to stock milk-free products and some supermarkets stock a limited range of such items. Avoid yoghurt, cows' milk, butter and cheeses. Try soya milk.

WHEAT ALLERGY

For further information and advice on allergy to wheat, send a stamped, addressed envelope to: AAA (Action Against Allergy), PO Box 278, Twickenham, Middlesex TW1 4QQ. Tel: 020 8892 2711.

FAN OVENS

The best ovens are the conventional ones with a rising heat. Fan ovens have even heat at all levels. For this type of oven reduce centrigrade temperature by 20° and bake for about one-third less time than suggested in the recipes. As ovens vary from manufacturer to manufacturer, this is only a guide. You may need to experiment with your particular oven, which means a hit-and-miss approach to start with. Be sure to mark up the recipes with the correct temperature and time for your particular make of fan oven.

FREEZING

When putting food in your freezer, always label and date it. Have a regular spring-clean and discard food which has been in the freezer too long. It could be a health risk and will probably be a disappointment.

WHEAT-FREE SOY SAUCE

Usually soy sauce is made with soya beans and wheat flour. Tamari type soy sauce is made from soya beans and rice. (Note: Tamari is not a brand name, merely a type.) Your local health store may be able to supply you. As it keeps well, why not buy in bulk? Check lables carefully. Do not buy any brand which contains MSG.

ALLERGY GROUPS

There is probably an allergy support group in your area. They usually have local knowledge regarding shopping for special diets as well as mail order information and could provide you with useful information.

Approximate percentages of saturated and polyunsaturated fat in fats and oils

Fats/oils	% saturated fat	% polyunsaturated fat
● cream/butter	61	3
● suet	58	1
● lard	44	10
● hard margarine	38	16
● hard vegetable oil	38	16
★ polyunsaturated margarine	25	55
● egg yolk	38	11
● ice cream	67	3
† olive oil	15	12
● coconut oil	90	2
● palm oil	49	9
groundnut oil (peanut)	20	30
★ soya oil	15	60
★ sunflower seed oil	14	52
★ safflower seed oil	11	76
★ maize (corn) oil	17	52

★ good levels polyunsaturates
● highly saturated fats/oils
† high in monounsaturates

Liquid Conversions

IMPERIAL	METRIC	US CUPS
½ fl oz	15 ml	1 tbsp (level)
1 fl oz	30 ml	⅛ cup
2 fl oz	60 ml	¼ cup
3 fl oz	90 ml	⅜ cup
4 fl oz (¼ US pint)	125 ml	½ cup
5 fl oz (¼ UK pint)	150 ml	⅔ cup
6 fl oz	175 ml	¾ cup
8 fl oz (½ US pint)	250 ml	1 cup (½ pint)
10 fl oz (½ UK pint)	300 ml	1¼ cups
12 fl oz	375 ml	1½ cups
16 fl oz (1 US pint)	500 ml	2 cups (1 pint)
20 fl oz (1 UK pint)	600 ml	2½ cups
1½ pints	900 ml	3¾ cups
1¾ pints	1 litre	1 qt (4 cups)
2 pints (1 qt)	1¼ litres	1¼ quarts
2⅓ pints	1½ litres	3 US pints
3¼ pints	2 litres	2 quarts

Quantities are given in imperial measures, metric equivalents and US cups. Follow one set of measures, do not mix them.

US and UK pints are not the same: 1 UK pint = 20 fl oz; 1 US pint = 16 fl oz; 1 litre = 33 fl oz (1 US qt).

For the best results in the US and UK, use the oz and lbs measures and weights rather than using a cup measure or metric measures.

General Index

Recipe Index